Teaching Deaf Children
Techniques and Methods

◆

TEACHING DEAF CHILDREN
TECHNIQUES AND METHODS

◆

Danielle M. Sanders, Ph.D.
Department of Exceptional Education
University of Wisconsin–Milwaukee
Milwaukee, Wisconsin

A College-Hill Publication
Little, Brown and Company
Boston/Toronto/San Diego

College-Hill Press
A Division of
Little, Brown and Company (Inc.)
34 Beacon Street
Boston, Massachusetts 02108

Library of Congress CIP Number 87–23757

ISBN 0–316–77015–9

Printed in the United States of America

CONTENTS

Contents

Acknowledgments

There are many people I need to thank for their contributions to the preparation of this text.

First and foremost, I want to recognize and thank the individual who was my motivation for writing this text. My oldest son, Ron Sanders, Jr., was born profoundly deaf and successfully survived the struggle of raising hearing parents. I have learned as much from him as I have from the special education classes I took as a student.

A special "thank you" goes to two tireless people, Eileen Walsh and Roger Kocher, who typed and retyped this manuscript. In addition, Eileen and another graduate student, Jeannine Mawhinney, deserve thanks for allowing me to include material in this text that they prepared for my classes.

A very special note of appreciation goes to Janelle Pagelsdorf, whose extraordinary way with words helped to clarify my often unclear phrasing. As a secretary and a friend, her good-natured patience often must have been stretched to the limit. I am thoroughly grateful to her.

I want to thank my youngest son, Dustan, and my parents, Mr. & Mrs. Dan Hornett, who encouraged me at the beginning of this endeavor. Marie Linvill of College-Hill Press was the force behind the development stage. Finally, a very important person in my life, Philip Heffner, supported and lovingly prodded me through the final months, which somehow seemed the most difficult at times.

Preface

This book is designed to address the needs of dedicated individuals in teacher training programs who are preparing to meet the challenges of teaching hearing-impaired children. The primary goals that guided my effort were a desire to describe factors that affect and directly influence the overall development—linguistic, cognitive, social, emotional, and academic—of hearing-impaired children; to provide some perspective and understanding of the limitations imposed by a hearing impairment and the ramifications on the classroom and teacher; and finally, to provide practical applications of this knowledge and understanding in the preparation of materials and selection of teaching techniques and strategies necessary to implement appropriate programming for hearing-impaired children in the classroom. This text covers a gamut of materials on hearing impairment from family and psychosocial issues to cognition and language development to planning and implementing lessons.

This book focuses on the needs of hearing-impaired children of hearing parents and on the problems that generally confront this specific group. I am aware that it appears that hearing-impaired children of deaf parents who use manual communication usually require different academic techniques due to the differences in early language input and its effects on development.

While writing this text, I tried to keep in mind what it was like for me in the classroom, and what I wish I had known then. I wanted to share the knowledge I acquired in my years as a classroom teacher and the satisfaction I have experienced teaching children with hearing impairments.

Considerations in the Education of Hearing-Impaired Children

When hearing children face school for the first time, they are equipped for learning. That is, they possess all the processes required to benefit from the educational experience. The children cannot read, nor can they think critically, but all of the internal equipment needed to execute these skills is in place. Hearing children have already acquired, in a natural manner, the language and cognitive structures necessary for symbolization, which will make them efficient learners.

On the other hand, when hearing-impaired children enter school, they are seldom equipped with the preknowledge and mental abilities that are the basis for the kind of education that is normally provided by school systems. Profound loss of hearing at birth or at an early age deprives a child of sensory input, ultimately affecting the child's overall social, emotional, and mental development. Thus, potential for academic success may be hampered by language limitations and resultant consequences.

Despite these limitations, hearing-impaired children are entitled to the same educational opportunities as their hearing peers. The objectives of education for hearing-impaired children should be the same as those desired by our society for all children. Hearing-impaired children, like hearing children, are entitled to the best education their community can provide. As stated by the Educational Policies Commission of the National Education Association, objectives of education include the following.

1. *Self-realization.* This is the achievement of self-efficiency, in accordance with the potential of an individual, in acquiring knowledge of how to use mental, physical, social, and emotional characteristics and how to recognize strengths and cope with limitations.

2. *Human relationships.* This is the achievement of human interactions conducive to a give-and-take relationship between the individual and the environment.

3. *Economic efficiency.* This is the attainment of the qualities of workmanship, knowledge, flexibility, and the judgment necessary for economic independence.

4. *Civic responsibility.* This is the attainment of the ability

to participate effectively in the social and political aspects of our culture.

Thus, the overall goal of education is to prepare individuals, handicapped or nonhandicapped, to live as successfully as possible within society. The attainment of this goal demands a dedication to the development of a total program for individual hearing-impaired children.

Perhaps the most influential factor in hearing-impaired children's academic performance is educational intervention. For obvious reasons, it is not practical to attempt to teach hearing-impaired children in the same manner, with the same materials, or at the same rate as hearing children. A hearing impairment presents educational problems that are unique. Therefore, the instructional practices and programs designed for the classroom should also be unique. Any program for hearing-impaired children should be designed to meet the special needs of students who are handicapped socially and educationally by their hearing impairment. Considerations for program planning that will allow children to attain educational objectives at the highest level of their individual abilities is critical. Dedicated, quality teachers must be highly trained to assume the special responsibilities for all aspects of their students' development. This includes modifying the learning environment and the educative process so that each hearing-impaired child can learn effectively, as well as providing a warm, accepting atmosphere that will enhance a child's self-esteem.

In planning such a program, we must examine other factors

in addition to the language limitation. For example, we need to consider individual differences in the degree of hearing loss, the age of onset, the age at which intervention began, and the etiology of the hearing impairment, along with family makeup, family acceptance of the handicap, self-concept, and social competence. These individual factors must be recognized in each student and accounted for in educational programming.

Family Concerns

Of primary importance in any child's overall development is the parents' acceptance of and attitude toward the child. Parental approval strongly influences a child's emotional and behavioral characteristics. It has long been recognized by professionals that the identification of deafness in an infant or toddler, especially in a hearing family, precipitates a serious family crisis. In most cases, the birth of a deaf child is the family's first contact with deafness. According to Schein and Delk (1974), over 90 percent of hearing-impaired children are born to hearing parents. At the moment of the diagnosis, whether at birth or at a later age, the parents, in essence, experience the "death" of their perfect child. Parents often feel personal guilt and may try to place blame, or they may experience periods of panic, uncertainty, and despondency. News of a deaf child has an overwhelming impact on siblings as well as the extended family. Typically, mothers seem to suffer more often from guilt, sorrow, mourning, and anger, interfering with a warm, stable relationship with the infant. The mother-infant relationship is one of the most important factors, in terms of infant development, both psychologically and physically.

At the time of diagnosis, there exists a major family crisis with little time to prepare for it. The entire family unit suffers as the parents struggle in an effort to readjust and stabilize their world. Accomodation to the hearing loss and its concomitant considerations forces change in the lives of all the family members. Parents of handicapped children reportedly go through a grieving process that includes denial, guilt, helplessness, anger, and, finally, acceptance. According to Cohen (1980), if parents fail to come to terms with their feelings, they may react by denying the handicap exists, thereby further disrupting relationships between the child and other family members. Unfortunately, reaching the acceptance stage does not bring final resolution to the crisis: even after acceptance, the handicap must be dealt with on a daily basis. For all who work with hearing-impaired children and their families in any capacity, an important point to remember is that total and final acceptance of the handicap is never accomplished once and for all. Feelings of despair, sorrow, and anger recur continuously as new experiences happen in the life of the handicapped child. How the parents react to these crises is of primary importance in the child's psychological adjustment.

Common responses by parents include overprotection, forced compensation, and outright rejection of their children. Frequently, parents are afraid to let their child explore the environment and do things that other children do because of fear for

their child's safety. They are often more permissive and accepting of inappropriate behavior than they would be with their
hearing children. Predictably, these reactions stunt the child's
emotional growth and development of independence.

Too often, the parents' inability to accept the handicap leads
to a hopeless, expensive search for cures or for the right hearing
aid. Unfortunately, there is no magic available that will make
a deaf child into a hearing child. The search for miracles can
translate into a powerful negative message to the child that is
totally destructive to the self-concept. "We'll love you on the
condition that you hear or at least act hearing." The child will
receive the negative message but will not be able to understand
why it was sent.

In addition, to uninformed parents, the hearing impairment
may seem like a speech problem. Therefore, it may seem
reasonable to them that once the child learns to talk, all will
be normal. This misunderstanding can be compounded and
extended by professionals who give false hopes to the parents,
thereby postponing the acceptance period.

As mentioned earlier, adjustment to a hearing impairment
is a lifelong process for the child and family. Deafness is never
accepted once and for all; new problems and adjustments are
forced on everyone as the child matures. There are constant emotional problems for the child and parents because the child is
"different," compounded by the continuous presence of special,
often misunderstood needs. There appear to be three critical
periods in the life cycle (Meadow, 1973) that can cause a recur-
rence of fear and concern for parents and that may produce crises
periods in family members' lives. The first is the time of diagnosis.

The response of the parents to the diagnosis is extremely important to the child's growth in the area of identity and personality development. Once the initial shock of diagnosis subsides, the family can concentrate on providing a quality life for the hearing-impaired child and others in the home. Parents and family members strive to retain some sense of normalcy in their lives; however, the preschool years are filled with reminders of the child's "differentness." Parents face well-meant but often contradictory advice from specialists as well as family members. Communication limitations requiring the need for constant language stimulation, explaining the hows and whys of the environment, and providing discipline all take a tremendous amount of time and put additional demands on daily family life.

The second crisis period occurs when the child reaches school age, which is often younger than usual. Further adaptations must be made in the family life as parents struggle with the opposing goals of providing protection and independence for their hearing-impaired child. Parents tend to shelter and over-protect their hearing-impaired children from the harshness of the real world, which only serves to delay the resolution of the autonomy crisis through which children normally proceed. Additionally, many hours are spent with homework as parents try to support school activities. Often, journals and daily logs are kept and sent back and forth to school, which means parents essentialy become teacher aides in attempts to provide necessary skills for their children to learn and compete in school. The amount of school involvement increases as children go from first grade to higher grades.

Puberty brings the third critical period. As adolescence

approaches, a whole new set of problems and concerns arise, from pimples and dating to self-awareness and sexuality. These normal phenomena can cause distress and disruption in any family as the mood swings that often accompany preadolescence alter interpersonal attitudes and exchanges. It is at this important time in life that hearing-impaired children struggle with establishing their own identities, while recognizing their differences. At this time, hearing-impaired children begin to feel isolated from their hearing peers, and self-concept becomes hampered by the lack of deaf models. There is often a conflict in the identity crisis, which involves choosing more frequent interaction in the deaf world or the hearing world. Deaf adolescents finally realize they will not become hearing as they grow older. The comfortableness of the ease of communication offered by the deaf culture often conflicts with the parents' hopes and expectations that they will live and function entirely in the hearing community. Hearing-impaired children who belong to minority ethnic groups have additional identity concerns. Ideally, a healthy, successful resolution of these conflicts would allow an individual to function well within several worlds. An unsuccessful resolution will place individuals in a position that can alienate them from any world. Adolescence is normally a time of confusion, exclusion, and misunderstanding. A positive sense of self-worth is important to good mental health. Individuals need to feel accepted and comfortable with peers of both sexes. It is during adolescence that feelings of future adequacies as a sexual partner and parent come into focus. Many parents don't know how to deal effectively with the conflicts inherent in adolescence.

It is also at this time that parents confront the hazards that lie ahead for their hearing-impaired children as they approach adulthood. The parents become concerned with future prospects in the areas of postsecondary schooling, vocational choices, marriage partners, leisure time, money, and becoming active participants within the community.

Not only do hearing-impaired adolescents lack the ability and means to express themselves to many other people, but they are also restricted in receiving explanations as to what comprises acceptable social behavior. Thus, deaf children can be left in a state of confusion about what is expected of them. They not only fail to make themselves understood, but they also fail to understand the rules and restrictions of family and society.

Psychosocial Issues

Not only do family practices and attitudes toward the handicap affect the emotional development of hearing-impaired children, but society's acceptance plays an important role as well. Generally, very little is known by the public about deafness and its accompanying problems. The fact that a deaf child is born without a major sensory path is as invisible to the mind as it is to the eye. The hearing-impaired child must not only struggle with learning social routines and accepted behavior, but he or she also must deal with the misconceptions, stereotyping, and prejudices of society. Social functioning is complex and confusing as it differs depending on the circumstances and the individuals involved in any context.

The overall social development of hearing-impaired children differs from that of hearing children in the range of social opportunities for the expression and practice of skills. It is important to remember that due to personal differences and family experiences, some hearing-impaired individuals will cope and adjust to their disability more successfully than others. The manner and degree of successful coping will determine emotional and social maturity. Unfortunately, parents often feel inadequate in providing the means with which the child can develop socially acceptable behavior. The child then must provide his or her own analysis of the situation, which can be inadequate or inappropriate (Davis, 1974).

Deafness influences and modifies behavior in many ways by altering modes of perceptual experience and organization (Myklebust, 1964; Vernon, 1969). Previously, studies in personality development and cultural patterning of the deaf have indicated a "deaf personality" stereotype (Levine, 1960), containing these principle features: (1) emotional immaturity; (2) rigidity; (3) social/cultural impoverishment; and (4) narrow intellectual functioning. Without special attention to the specific needs of hearing-impaired children, this stereotype can become a self-fulfilling prophecy. In order to develop into socially mature persons and to realize their full potential, hearing-impaired children must have quantities of information about social customs, habits, and usage (Dicker, 1977). They also require sufficient opportunities to enjoy a variety of social and interpersonal relationships in which to practice this information and knowledge. They must be encouraged to seek out experiences that will give them the sophistication needed to deal successfully with real life situations (Dicker, 1977). How deaf children are treated in social situations is critical to their developing self-image (Davis, 1974). Repeated successful experiences will aid in the attainment of a positive self-concept.

Children learn to manipulate their environments. With hearing children, this is done through vocalizations as they experiment and learn acceptable and effective ways to obtain what they desire. Hearing children learn to manipulate their environment successfully through language and communication. They learn why something is unsuccessful, and they learn how to remediate the reasons for failure. With limited language and communicative abilities, hearing-impaired children resort to other means, usually by acting out, which is viewed as unacceptable by society. If children do not receive feedback indicating these actions are inappropriate, negative behaviors will be reinforced. They will continue to use these actions and will become conditioned to act in immature ways in order to manipulate their environment. If these behaviors continue for any length of time, it will become difficult, if not impossible, to extinguish the unwanted behaviors and to teach acceptable ones. Without education about acceptable behaviors at an early age, hearing-impaired children will begin to deviate from what is considered acceptable as they are unable to direct themselves into age-appropriate, socially acceptable behavior. These differences have a tendency to increase as children get older. Finally, the children themselves will reach a point when they recognize that their behavior is not the same as their siblings or hearing peers, but they will be unable to communicate and therefore understand these differences. This results in frustration, which serves to feed the inappropriate behaviors, which in turn causes more self-doubt and cultivates negative feelings of self-worth.

Unfortunately, hearing-impaired children often miss the opportunity to communicate freely with parents and peers. This results in consequences detrimental to their emotional development. As previously presented information indicates, outlets for venting frustration, disappointments, curiosity, and anger are limited, and emotions are often expressed in physically inappropriate and immature behaviors. As a result, undue stress and strain is placed on mental and physical health. Imagine, if you can, being forced to keep your feelings, thoughts, and questions bottled up inside because of the lack of a communication system through which you can converse.

Children with speech or language disorders are significantly handicapped and therefore appear to be at risk of developing associated behavioral problems. Several studies (Jensema & Trybus, 1978; Meadow & Trybus, 1979; Quigley & Kretschmer, 1982; Schlesinger & Meadow, 1972) suggest that a deaf child's early experiences precipitate a higher rate of behavioral and emotional disorders in school-age hearing-impaired children than in school-age hearing children. It is further suggested that this is the result of disturbed parent-child interactions, impoverished socialization and experiential opportunities, and a disruption in the personality structure development. Studies concerning the prevalence of emotional disturbance within the hearing-impaired population began as early as 1938 (Cohen, 1980).

However, it has only been in the last 15 years that serious attempts to identify the frequency of occurrence have been undertaken. The results of these studies vary, but they generally indicate that a relatively high proportion of hearing-impaired students have emotional problems. The incidence ranges from approximately 8 percent (Schildroth, 1980) to 19 percent (Gentile & McCarthy, 1973) of children involved in these studies. The degree of variance is understandable when considering the difficulties intrinsic to such studies. For example, many tests used in the research rely heavily on verbal or written responses. In addition, an important factor to consider is the subjectiveness of the researcher's judgment. The interpretation of what is acceptable or unacceptable behavior, or what is significant or insignificant, is up to the professional conducting the research (Cohen, 1980).

However, it is safe to assume that the lack of verbal skills and the communication limitations in some families will contribute to the emotional and behavioral development of deaf children. Language is considered the primary means used to internalize experience (Myklebust, 1964). Therefore, it follows that when language is restricted, there may be a reciprocal restriction in the ability to integrate experience. Myklebust wrote that the lack of sound makes the experiences of hearing-impaired children qualitatively different from those of hearing individuals.

Educational Achievement

The degree of achievement by deaf children in academic areas falls well below that of their hearing peers. We need to remember that deaf children are dependent on formal instruction to learn the things that hearing children learn in a casual, infor-mal, almost incidental manner. An educational retardation of 2 to 5 years has consistently been documented by researchers comparing the achievement test results of hearing and hearing-impaired children (Quigley & Kretschmer, 1982). As could be expected, the gap widens as the children grow older.

So much is communicated in written form that the ability to read is the key to the educational and social development of deaf children. Studies have revealed that, on the average, only 5 percent of deaf children in special schools or classes read at a 10th grade level or better at age 16 (Trybus & Karchmer, 1977). A much higher proportion, 60 percent, read at a level below sixth grade, and approximately 30 percent are functionally illiterate when they leave school. The most often quoted mean reading level for hearing-impaired persons 20 years old or older is a 4.5 grade level. DiFrancesca (1972) reported that the average reading growth was 0.2 grade levels per year of schooling.

Other studies have indicated that at age 9, hearing-impaired children in the mainstream function academically 1.5 years behind their hearing classmates; at age 14, they function more than 5 years behind. Furthermore, hearing-impaired children often remain outside of full social interaction because they leave school unable to meet the demands that this kind of interac-tion requires.

Summary

A hearing impairment is a functional disorder, and, as such, it affects the person's total environment, not just his or her hearing. It affects emotional, social, and mental development. The primary job of the school is the development of language and communication skills that hearing children learn in a natural manner. Additionally, the goal of education should be to enable the deaf person to live as full a life as possible. Usually, this means literacy; however, if this is unrealistic due to individual levels of ability, then the goal should be functional self-sufficiency. Based on the unique education problems that deafness creates, educational programs designed to ameliorate these problems should also be unique.

Deafness creates a language deficit that interferes with the acquisition and processing of knowledge. Communication skills are the tools of education. To succeed in any academic area, a child must have reading skills, and language is a prerequisite. Therefore, if deaf children are to learn, they must have help through the entire educational process. This puts the onus on teachers and the educational system.

When hearing-impaired children are educated among hearing children, differences that are characteristic of all children and that affect learning are compounded by differences in the degree and the onset of deafness as well as family and societal expectations and acceptance. These differences must be recognized and dealt with to facilitate education. Every teacher must attempt to tailor learning experiences to each child's cognitive, physical, social, and emotional level. An obvious consideration is the language level and communication functioning of each child. These are considered in the next chapter.

CHAPTER
· 2 ·

Deafness, Cognition, and Language Development

*I*n order to examine the learning process and academic potential of hearing-impaired children, we must first look at cognitive development and the link between cognition and language, along with the interrelationship of cognition, language, and the roles that impaired hearing plays in the development of each.

It has been common to find hearing-impaired children testing in the retarded range on full-scale scores of IQ tests. This has brought up questions of the relationship between hearing impairment and intelligence. Hearing-impaired children score lowest on verbal sections of tests. This is due to the requirement of high verbal mediation, directions, or responses in the verbal subtests. However, performance scores are are usually within the normal IQ range. Based on this information and with knowledge of the demands of academic achievement, it is not surprising to find that, overall, hearing-impaired children consistently fall below their hearing peers in academic areas.

Before we can consider these issues, however, it is necessary to define terms as they are to be used within the context of this book.

Hearing impaired is the umbrella term that encompasses all degrees of hearing loss—from slight to profound. Therefore, all deaf people are hearing impaired, though not all hearing-impaired people are deaf. Throughout this book, *hearing impaired* will be used because it includes all people with hearing problems, not only those with severe to profound losses, as the term *deaf* denotes.

The term *hard-of-hearing* is used to describe hearing impairment that adversely affects a child's educational performance. Hard-of-hearing individuals are functional for ordinary life purposes, usually with the help of a hearing aid (Stout, 1982).

Deafness is a condition in which perceivable sounds, including speech, have no meaning for ordinary life purposes, even with the help of a hearing aid (Stout, 1982).

Cognitive Development

First of all, we need to define what is meant by *cognition*. The best overall definition describes *cognition* as "the various modes of knowing, perceiving, remembering, imagining, conceiving, judging, and reasoning" (Nicolosi, Harryman, & Kresheck, 1980).

Historically, there have been three basic orientations concerning the intellectual capacity and mental development of deaf persons. The earliest perspective, which was held until the mid 1940s, viewed the deaf as deficient or significantly inferior in their cognitive abilities. This view was substantiated primarily by the consistently lower performances exhibited by deaf people on IQ and achievement tests. Generally, the deaf demonstrate a 2-year deficit on intelligence tests and a 5-year deficit on academic tests when compared with hearing persons. For this reason, researchers such as Pintner (1933) believed that, in the cognitive area, the deaf as a group are qualitatively, as well as quantitatively, different from hearing people and that the differences are inherent in deafness. This view automatically implies that the differences cannot be changed or remediated as they are an integral part of the biological makeup of deafness. On a positive note, Pintner found that the deaf excelled in mechanical and motor ability and concrete intelligence. Based on these findings, he recommended an emphasis on mechanical, motor, and concrete activities in the educational programming for deaf children.

The second perspective suggested the deaf were not intellectually inferior but, rather, had considerable qualitative differences. This perspective viewed deaf individuals as persons who could deal with reality only on a concrete level. One proponent of this bio-social orientation, which lasted from the mid 1940s to the late 1960s was Myklebust (1964). He considered the conceptual disparity between the hearing and the deaf to be due to the limitations that hearing impairment imposed on language development. Myklebust considered average language develop ment necessary for the average development of psychological processes and learning. He proposed that, due to the effects of the sensory deprivation of deafness, which impaired the acquisition of language, the mental growth and intellectual functioning of deaf children would not parallel that of hearing children. Myklebust presumed that all preverbal experiences of deaf children had to differ considerably from those of hearing infants because the deaf children did not experience audition. Thus, according to Myklebust, all nonverbal behavior, including perceptual processes, was therefore established and structured differently in deaf individuals; auditory input, with which humans monitor the environment, and which is defective in the hearing-impaired, alters experience (Myklebust, 1964).

Our brain takes information from our senses and integrates it into meaningful units and stores it. Experiences are organized and stored in ways that enable us to recall these experiences and allow us to make educated guesses about the possible outcomes of new situations based on what has happened in the past. It seems apparent that visual information is coded differently than auditory information (Tomlinson-Keasey & Kelly, 1974). This means that not only will experiences be perceived differently, but the processing of the information and schematic organization will also differ in hearing-impaired people. Therefore, it can be hypothesized that if the schematic organization is different, then there is the possibility that memory functions will be altered as well.

In addition, child development experts such as Piaget (1974) stressed the significance of sensory input as the foundation for intelligence. One who completely lacks auditory stimulation and experience will also have deficits in the abiltiy to symbolize, which is a function of verbalization. This implies that with the preclusion of normal language development, standard mental development will not occur.

The third orientation, which began in the late 1960s and has continued through the present, denies the idea of an inherent cognitive deficit. Rather, it views the deaf as normal in the area of cognitive skills and supports the concept that thinking processes in the deaf and hearing are similar. Supporters of this theory include Rosenstein, Vernon, and Furth (Moores, 1987). This perspective considers that the only differences exhibited in the cognitive abilities of the deaf are found primarily in the developmental timetable. Studies that support this view are based on controlling the linguistic factors in testing along with examining the concept development of hearing impaired children on the Piagetian framework, particularly during the sensorimotor period.

The Relationship of Language and Cognition

In order to understand the relationship of language and cognition, we must first define specific words. *Language* is defined here as any accepted, structured symbolic system used for inter- or intrapersonal communication; *speech* is considered to be the motor act of verbal expression (the spoken system). *Verbal* refers to any way of dealing with words, including expressive or receptive means, whether spoken, written, or gestures, including sign language and finger-spelling. *Vocal* pertains to use of the voice, speech, or organs of speech, and *conceptual thinking* refers to the organization or structuring of ideas or meanings from experience.

Based on the results of studies of the mental functioning of the hearing-impaired when linguistic input and responses are controlled, hearing-impaired people's deficiencies would seem to be based on language impoverishment. Furth's (1966) studies have suggested that thinking is independent from language, at least up to the concrete operations stage, during which time children begin to develop the ability to apply logical thought to concrete problems. The formal operational period, in which abstract thought processes emerge, is seriously delayed or never reached by deaf children resulting in individuals who are unable to function beyond the concrete level. In other words, the hearing-impaired child who never attains the formal operations stage will not be able to handle abstract concepts. Furth (1966a) suggested that three reasons hearing-impaired children did more poorly than hearing children on tests: (1) experimenter/tester bias; (2) the language deprivation of the hearing-impaired; and (3) the social deprivation of the hearing-impaired. Furth emphasized the value of thought, suggesting that with the ability to think critically, all other problems confronted by the deaf could be solved. He further suggested that the rigidity (the inability to shift) often demonstrated by hearing-impaired persons was partly due to the failure of the schools to teach them to think. He felt that hearing-impaired children were deprived of exposure to thinking skills and suffered from a lack of input, exacerbating their innate processing problems and leading to their concrete thinking behavior. Based on this, Furth proposed that teaching hearing-impaired children to think should take priority over language instruction in the classroom.

Piaget was a proponent of the view that language develops from thought. He felt that language plays a minor role in early cognitive development and, therefore, that deaf children should pass through the sensorimotor stage in the same manner and at the same rate as hearing children, given adequate environmental stimulation. During the sensorimotor period, children develop certain structures that will be crucial to later developing modes of thought and language. Included among these early structures are causality; an elementary understanding of gravity, spatial, and object relations; proper social behavior; and problem-solving. Direct interaction with the environment and the feedback the child receives from this interaction results in the completion of the sensorimotor period of development and provides the basis for symbolization. Symbolic thought develops as the child learns to manipulate reality internally and thus gains the ability to use language symbols. This in turn allows the child to use language, which serves to enhance the development of the intellectual structures rather than determining their emergence. Intellectual development proceeds from a symbolic level of play and imitation, through concrete operations, and on to the higher operations. It appears then that language plays a more important role in higher operations. That is, the more abstract the concepts, the more related they are to language. The ability to use symbolization or imagery allows more complex thinking to occur.

Myklebust (1948), on the other hand, felt that language governed thought. He developed a theoretical hierarchy of experience ranging from the concrete stage to the abstract stage; however, these stages must be considered to be overlapping rather than discrete.

The following definitions are important for a complete understanding of Myklebust's hierarchy: *Experience* refers to the participation in an activity or event and forms the base for the eventual attainment of concepts. *Sensation* refers to the activity of the nervous system resulting from the activation of any given sense organ. *Perception* is defined as the interpretation of a sensation, which involves discrimination, identification, and recognition, and which is then translated into a meaningful and coherent picture of the environment. *Imagery* involves a pictographic and/or ideographic mental image. *Verbal symbolic* behavior is unique to humans; it includes the ability to make language possible. *Language* is an arbitrary symbol system used to represent, communicate, and exchange ideas, feelings, and thoughts. It is abstract in that it does not require that the experience, object, circumstance, or stimuli be present. With verbal symbolization comes the ability to internalize and communicate with others. *Conceptualization* is the process by which we classify and categorize experience. It is the formation of a concept or an ideal. Conceptualization does not seem to be limited to verbal symbolic functioning but appears to be highly dependent on it. Myklebust's hierarchy can be shown as follows:

5. conceptualization
4. verbal symbolization (language)
3. imagery
2. perception
1. sensation

---

experience

Myklebust considered this hierarchy to be reciprocal in nature. This means that if one area is disturbed, as with sensation in the case of deafness, all above it will be altered to some degree. He suggested that the language problems of the deaf stemmed from two causes: a different experiential base than hearing children plus a limited contact with the language itself.

Deaf children receive sensations differently from hearing children; therefore, it seems probable that his perceptions are developed differently; and, therefore, imagery symbols and concepts will be structured differently. The levels of symbolization and conceptualization will be most affected, impeding the development of certain types of abstract behavior. Deaf children, especially those with profound deafness from birth, are highly dependent of visual imagery, affecting the extent to which they are able to abstract.

Another researcher who supported the concept of language governing the development of thought processes and the growth of the mind was Whorf (1956). He proposed the concepts of "linguistic determinism," which refers to his theory that all higher levels of thinking are dependent on language, and "linguistic relativity," which proposes that language varies from culture to culture. Whorf suggested that by studying and analyzing languages of different cultures, and comparing them with the differences in thinking within different cultures, we would gain information about what language contributes to thinking.

Language Development

The acquisition of language has traditionally been examined in terms of nature theory, which is based on what children bring with them biologically in terms of the learning task, or nurture theory, which takes into account the role of the environment.

Nature theory is based on the assumption that language is innately and physiologically predetermined. According to this viewpoint, language development is related to the growth of the human brain and is a direct result of maturation rather than of experience or learning. Nature theory suggests a critical period for learning language that is consistent across cultures and is generally considered to be between birth and 4 years of age.

A behavioral or nurture point of view is based on the stimulus-response theory, which states the acquisition of language occurs due to the rewards the child obtains when he or she initiates or tries to imitate adult language models. This theory assumes language is learned entirely through experience and interaction with the environment. Although studies substantiate that children do imitate what they hear, children also produce variations of models and speak original sentences. For instance, some studies have shown that children often ignore correct adult models and continue to make the same errors time and again. Thus, the nurture model fails to completely account for acquisition of language by children.

Due to the unanswered questions left by each theory, but recognizing the validity of certain assumptions within each, it seems logical to agree that innate ability and the environment must somehow interact and interrelate in the development of language.

The Relationship Between Cognition and Language in the Deaf

Considering all of the previously presented information, it appears reasonable to conclude that hearing-impaired children will acquire an inadequate language system. One researcher, Conrad (1979) suggested that by school age, even hard-of-hearing children may have sustained enough neurological deficit to impair untilization of linguistic information received exclusively through auditory pathways. In order to understand this acquisition of language, we need first to look at how language is acquired by hearing children.

Hearing children do not learn their language and culture through formal teaching processes. Instead, these are learned casually and incidentally by the children through continuous exposure to speech and its accompanying physical experiences in the home and community. Language is thus learned effectively without conscious effort through the interaction of the child's auditory sense and the environment. The development of this speech and language has usually reached a fairly high level of sophistication by the time the children are ready to enter school.

Let us contrast this easy acquisition of language by hearing children to the difficult task of learning language by hearing-impaired children. The child who is totally deaf from birth or before the age of 2 will never acquire any meaningful auditory receptive language. Consequently, auditory memory and auditory vocabulary will not be stored in the cortex. Such a hearing-impaired child is denied access to the meaningful spoken input that provides the necessary data and language base available to the hearing child.

The totally deaf child must rely primarily on visual and tactile clues to process the world. During his or her first 2 years, the child will develop sensorimotor structures that do not include auditory ways of processing and organizing the environment (Tomlinson-Keasey & Kelly, 1974). Auditory output becomes meaningless and decreases significantly at about 10 months of age (Lenneberg, 1967). The babbling behavior that results in speech in hearing children at this age fails to develop in deaf children. Hearing children attach spoken symbols to mental images. In this way, language is developed. Deaf children of deaf parents have been shown to have the ability to attach visual symbols to mental images; thus, signs and gestures become a feedback system for processing information and the language of signs is developed. This all indicates that language acquisition and the ability to use language will be different for the hearing and the hearing-impaired child.

By nature of their impairment, profoundly hearing-impaired

children must depend on distorted speech, speech patterns, and confusing lip movements in order to develop the auditory-vocal process known as language. For most of these children, even to acquire a limited oral communication system, they must undergo long, intensive tutoring sessions accompanied by much frustration and hard work. Due to their sensory impairment, these children must depend on vision for learning language. This dependency results in a major overall delay of speech and language development.

The ability to make sense of sounds is a critical aspect of learning language. The environment is full of sounds other than speech sounds, and the child's first task is to learn to distinguish between speech and other sounds. Once this has been done, there are other vital aspects of language that the child must be able to sort out and understand. For example, language consists of rules that are not explicitly stated; the hearing child soon learns to recognize these rules through trial and error. Most profoundly or totally deaf children, on the other hand, must be formally taught the rules with practice drills. Language becomes a lesson, and the normal interactive process becomes virtually nonexistant. The hearing-impaired child's rate of acquisition becomes dependent on the opportunities deliberately provided for practice by parents and teachers.

General Findings in Language of the Deaf

We have already determined that there is a discrepancy between the language abilities of the hearing and the hearing-impaired. Several studies have examined and analyzed, in detail, the production and comprehension of language by hearing-impaired children. Instead of concentrating on specific studies and examining them one by one, we will look at the general conclusions of the studies first and then examine the implications for the classroom.

Studies of deaf childrens' language acquisition suggest that it parallels that of hearing children, although there is a definite delay. As we shall see later, this delay gradually widens as the children grow older; this is where modifying and adapting materials used in our classrooms becomes urgent. The components of language that have been studied include lexicon, semantics, phonology, and pragmatics. Although the sensory impairment precludes the capacity to receive language, hearing-impaired children somehow acquire, at least partially, the rules that control our language.

An analysis by Quigley and Power (1972) of typical language production of hearing-impaired children attending special schools revealed the following characteristics:

1. Word length does not differ, although the sentences of the hearing-impaired are shorter than those of hearing children.

2. The use of complex sentences is developmentally delayed.

3. Writing is often in a rigid, stereotypic style.

4. The hearing-impaired children used more determiners,

nouns, and verbs than hearing children and fewer adverbs, auxiliaries, and conjunctions.

Developmental analysis of the kinds of errors in written production showed the following:

1. Omission of words necessary to make grammatically correct sentences, particularly function words (most frequent error)

2. Substitution of wrong words

3. Addition of unnessary words

4. Word order other than standard English

The acquisition of syntax progressed through developmental stages, with the deaf children reaching stages at a much slower rate than their hearing peers. Interestingly, many deaf children seemed to acquire syntactic structures peculiar to themselves (Bernstein & Tiegerman, 1985). These structures also appeared in the writing of deaf students, which suggests that they follow some sort of rule pattern; that is, these structures are thought to be generated by rules due to their consistency. When confronted with the task of interpreting complex sentences, deaf children tend to convert the sentences into a subject-verb-object (S-V-O) sentence pattern; therefore, the sentences were misunderstood. For example, the sentence, "The boy bit the girl and ran home," would be understood by deaf children as, "The girl ran home." Most research indicates that syntax is learned in the same sequence by both hearing and deaf children, while other research shows it is not. The key seems to be the degree of hearing loss (Quigley & Power, 1979).

In a review of earlier studies (Brannon & Murray, 1966; Power & Quigley, 1973; Quigley, Smith, & Wiler, 1974) examining syntactic and semantic development in deaf and hard-of-hearing children, Bernstein and Tiegerman (1985) reported on structure acquisition. The following structures are listed in the order of easiest to most difficult in the acquisition by deaf children:

negation

conjunction

question formation

pronomilization

verb processes

complimentation

relativization

For hearing children, the order of the easiest to most difficult structures is slightly different:

question formation

conjunction

negation

pronomilization

complimentation

relativization

verb processes

In the deaf and hard-of-hearing, the most well-established structures were negation, question forms, and conjunction, but even these were acquired to a lesser degree than in hearing children. The hard-of-hearing children demonstrated more problems with syntax than hearing children, while the deaf children exhibited more significant differences in language acquisition. Again, the variable that seems to be the deciding factor is the degree of hearing loss.

Reed (1986) reported that hearing-impaired children have a tendency to omit function words in sentences, which gives their speech telegraph-like characteristics. They tend to display great difficulty with the endings of verbs and with noun forms. Particularly difficult are past tense markers and the third-person singular forms. Present progressive appears to be the easiest tense for hearing-impaired children to achieve. Expressively, these children tend to use fewer words and more limited types of words than do hearing children.

Kretschmer and Kretschmer (1978) reported numerous errors or departures from standard English that produced deviant sentence structures. They also reported that deaf children demonstrate a limited mastery of the use of auxiliary verbs, confusion and misuse of determiners, and several errors in nominalization and relativization. Deaf children's speech characteristically is produced in a simple, simple construction.

Analysis of language samples by researchers demonstrated that the overall language of hearing-impaired children shows a reduction in both the overall number of words understood and the degree to which individual words are understood. Hearing-impaired children do not learn vocabulary at the same rate as hearing children; vocabulary comprehension may lag as much as 2 or 3 years behind. Evidence indicates that this gap tends to widen as the children get older. Additionally, they do not achieve age-appropriate language comprehension skills as they grow older. Time concepts appear to be more difficult to understand than space concepts (Kretschmer & Kretschmer, 1978). Function words, such as demonstrative pronouns, auxiliary verbs, and connectives are often lacking in their expressive vocabulary. Due to these problems, there have been suggestions that deaf children are deficient in the semantic notions that underlie oral language. However, this does not seem to be the case generally, as deaf children of deaf parents who use sign language as their first, natural form of language seem to acquire similar semantic relations as young hearing children. All studies, whether the population has been oral deaf children or those who use total communication, indicate that hearing-impaired children exhibit a delay in development of semantic abilities.

Deaf and hard-of-hearing children often tend to attach literal meanings to idiomatic, figurative, and slang expressions, resulting in significant problems with abstract language material. Although research has found the deaf to have problems understanding metaphors, they are not incapable of achieving some competency in this area. Instead, their problems may be due to the lack of exposure or lack of expectations for the use of metaphors. This suggests that the limitations may be more educationally based than hearing-loss based. (Reed, 1986).

The use of language in communication is another area in which deaf children suffer. Although early in their development deaf children tend to concentrate on the same set of semantic categories as hearing children, Kretschmer and Kretschmer emphasized that, traditionally, hearing-impaired children were taught linguistic principles through the use of isolated language exercises that resulted in a lack of knowledge of how to use the principles in conversation.

Deaf children show an inability to use connectors to maintain or change topics; they also have difficulty initiating conversations. Additionally, they seem to be unaware of breakdowns in communication and are unable to repair the breakdowns. They also seem to lack an understanding of the basic communication rules such as taking turns or when it is acceptable to interrupt.

Implications for Teaching

The various studies discussed provide sufficient evidence of the necessity for teachers to modify and adapt materials, techniques, and classroom environments in order to meet the language and cognitive needs of hearing impaired children. Once knowledge of deaf-specific syntactic structures is ascertained, along with specific structure use and misuse in individual children, remediation techniques can be developed and employed. One important consideration is to provide the student with the ability to generalize outside of the teaching situation. This requires that we do not treat the structures in isolation but rather as a meaningful part of a whole. Knowledge of the level and order of development will allow teachers to construct language and reading materials appropriate for each child. By accomodating the syntactic level of individual children, graduated remedial materials will allow them to attain increasing mastery of syntactic structures.

Teachers need to be cognizant of the specific pragmatic and semantic functions demonstrated by individual children within the communication system of the classroom. Vocabulary development that concentrates on expanding word meanings and the use of words outside of a restricted context should be two of the goals of a language program for hearing-impaired children.

It seems clear that language acquisition is a social process that must take place in the context of social interaction. Human infants are born with the capacity to develop patterned rules for appropriate language use from whatever input is provided within their environment. We must remember to emphasize language across all contexts for our students. Each activity should contain within it the potential for giving meaning to learning language.

Summary

The fact that a relationship exists between language and cognitive development is not questioned. Rather, it is the degree to which they are related that has been the source of inquiry and concern. Language impoverishment appears to be the most important factor in explaining the consistently lower scores of hearing-impaired children on intelligence tests. As teachers of the hearing-impaired, we must recognize that the ability to abstract, or use symbolization, is crucial to using language at a sophisticated level. Language, in turn, plays an important role in the development of higher level mental operations. A major concern for classroom application is the recognition of the stages of conceptual and language development in the preparation of the content, materials, and techniques we utilize in teaching.

Based on our knowledge of the inadequate language development in hearing-impaired children, we must concentrate on providing appropriate strategies and opportunities that will enable our students to achieve competency with language. Without adequate language capabilities, hearing-impaired students will continue to attach literal meanings to idiomatic, figurative, and slang expressions. This will affect their ability to socialize comfortably and severely limit their abilities to comprehend the written and spoken language used in the classroom. Academic and social failure will be the result of inadequate instructional provisions in the academic setting.

CHAPTER
· 3 ·

Strategies of Effective Teaching

*I*n order to be an effective teacher, you need to know where you are going in the classroom, and why. An important tool is a curriculum guide designed and adapted for use within each school district and based on the fundamental goals of educa-tion. The primary purpose of curriculum guides is to provide continuity throughout the school district in content areas. Teachers are expected to follow the guides in preparing and implementing their instructional programs so that the outcome of their educational intervention in the classroom is consistent with the stated goals of the curriculum. Teachers are responsi-ble for planning individual units and daily lessons that will allow students to attain the desired outcomes. Effective teachers need to be adept at formulating lesson plans that have purpose, meaning, and utility for deaf students at each stage of their development and that will guide students to reach long-term goals as well. Additionally, in order to accomplish their objectives, effective teachers must be able to motivate students and control classroom behavior to enable each student to realize his or her maximum potential.

Curricular Concerns

The primary function of a curriculum guide is to serve as a framework for instruction. A curriculum can be thought of as providing the process through which a child will be guided toward the attainment of long-range objectives in education, which are determined by society. Broadly defined, a curriculum can be said to be a systematic, sequential plan of activities, designed to achieve specific goals established by society's expectation that certain competencies be attained within the educational setting.

Each curriculum will reflect the organization of concepts and skills found within each general area and will usually contain suggestions for implementation, materials, and evaluation procedures. Typical curricula are established and accepted by specific school districts based on the assumption that when children enter school, they have already achieved certain skills and knowledge. Curricula are therefore usually designed to advance and build on previously learned skills and concepts.

To be effective, curricula should be dynamic—that is, in a constant state of revision, modification, and restructuring—to reflect our rapidly changing world. As technological and scientific advances are made, they must be incorporated into the educational program in order to assure that children are provided with the competencies required to function in an unknown, ever-changing future. It is reasonable to expect the curricula of the 1980s and 1990s to reflect implications of the space age. In addition, community and societal changes must be contained in curricula to keep up with changing times. For example, the changes in dating patterns, earlier sexual awareness, and chemical dependency must be discussed.

There are basically two types of curricula. The first, the *spiraling curriculum*, builds on previous information, lays the foundation for following information, and provides for interaction between the different levels of the curriculum. This form is based on the concept that new ideas can be presented to a young child and then gradually be increased in complexity and sophistication as the child matures. The spiral also allows learning to be specific to each individual child. The second type of curricula, the *layered curriculum*, provides information that is an end in itself within each level.

Unless employed by residential schools, which often function as school districts in themselves, teachers of the hearing-impaired will usually be required to work from curricula designed for hearing students. Although these may be useful in providing direction or information concerning what hearing children are exposed to, we must expect to make adaptations in order to make curricula appropriate for our students.

The first problem that we need to face is that, generally,

hearing-impaired children come to school with very limited information and a dearth of experiences; this combination automatically requires adaptation in the area of assumed prerequisite knowledge. A second concern is the linguistic deficit that hearing-impaired children exhibit. Together, these two problems usually render the prescribed regular education curriculum inappropriate for most of our students.

However, with some degree of adjustment, the content of the regular education curriculum can usually be followed successfully. We first need to eliminate extraneous material, which can cause confusion or sidetrack our intended outcomes. Adjustments must be made not only in what we teach, but also in how we teach. To enhance implementation of the curriculum, activities and sequencing must be age appropriate as well as ability related. Our adapted curricula should follow a comprehensive, systematic approach; contain specific goals and internal evaluative measures; and be diversified with a wide range of teaching appraisal techniques.

As we adapt and revise regular education curricula, several concerns need to be addressed: (1) methodology must emphasize the needs of deaf children and their unique learning styles; (2) goals must take into account the demands that society places on its members; (3) provisions must be made to reflect the scope and sequence for learning required skills, habits, and attitudes; (4) provision must be made for the development of an instructional program that has purpose, meaning, and utility for children at each stage of their development; and (5) each curriculum should provide concrete aids for teachers in terms of identifying the needs of children, setting instructional goals, and developing meaningful learning experiences.

Although curricula are designed to serve as guides to teachers, their outcomes and activities should not be considered all-inclusive and restricting. Minimally, curricula should contain the means for adaptation according to which track the students have been assigned: college-bound, vocational training, or self-sufficiency. Regardless of their level of functioning, hearing-impaired students will consistently meet problems that need to be solved in a socially acceptable manner. Therefore, when we adapt what is available, we must do it to provide appropriate, necessary experiences for the obtainment of the fundamental objectives of education while modifying the process so that all hearing-impaired students learn efficiently. Learning opportunities should be built into our unit plans and should be accessible daily to our students.

Developing Unit Plans

Just as curricula provide a general overall plan, units provide a framework for the achievement of smaller steps, or short-term objectives, which will eventually lead to the attainment of long-term goals. Each individual unit within specific content areas should contain a particular focus on a central theme and make use of its own resources and student experiences. Each unit, therefore, is a small part of the whole, which is designed to bring the student closer to the achievement of higher and more complex goals and a higher level of functioning. Units have no other intrinsic purpose than to function as a vehicle to move a child from his or her present point of development to a more sophisticated point.

Some units will be short, while others may be considerably longer and more extensive depending on content and objectives. For example, a unit designed to introduce the concept of the basic set in mathematics to young children will be longer in duration and contain more opportunities for exposure and practice than a unit designed to teach mixed fractions to upper elementary students who already understand the concept of like fractions. An important point to remember while planning is that units with the same title may have differing content and emphasis, based on the interests and needs of the students for whom the units have been developed.

Specific considerations when planning a unit include the following:

1. Units should be structured in terms of central themes or problems.

2. Units should be developed based on the interests, needs, and problems children will confront as they grow and mature.

3. Units should have relevance and purpose for the learners. If students can recognize the importance of the information and see that it has practical application, learning is maximized.

4. Units should be appropriate to the developmental level as well as the age of the learners.

5. Units should have clearly stated outcomes or goals that function as steps or guides to completing the units.

6. Units should be structured in such a way as to enable all students to participate and to share in their successful completion.

7. Units should offer several opportunities to use and reinforce previously learned skills and concepts.

8. Units should have a variety of activities that will determine your course of action that and are significantly related to the subject matter.

9. Units should include effective evaluative strategies to enable you to determine how effectively the material was learned by your students.

In sum, when planning a unit, the effective teacher will determine the learning needs of all the students involved, determine how those needs can best be met, and provide activities that will allow each student to achieve the desired outcomes most easily.

Effective Teachers

Before any learning can take place, certain prerequisites are required by the student. First, without having accepted his or her deafness, a deaf child will constantly be at odds with him- or herself and the teacher. The teacher's first priority then must be to help the child grow into a healthy, functioning adult by providing a warm, accepting environment where the child has successes rather than failures while learning. Too often, deaf children feel they have not been accepted or are not understood by their parents. Consciously or unconsciously, parents may send the message to their hearing-impaired children that they will be accepted only on the condition that they act hearing. This puts the children at an insurmountable disadvantage. The school then becomes the only place where the children can meet with success and finally learn to feel good about themselves.

When deaf students come to school with little self-confidence, the school—or rather the teacher—must provide areas in which they can acquire feelings of achievement and acceptance among their peers. Teachers must recognize and deal with the student's feelings of how they can relate what they learn in school to their own worth as members of their immediate environment. This requires that teachers develop sensitivity and skill in order to assist students in their psychosocial and educational adjustment. Teachers must assume the responsibility for developing techniques and materials that will allow all children a real opportunity for success in learning new tasks. By rewarding effort as well as mastery, opportunities for recognition and praise are provided. Deaf children need many experiences with positive reinforcement to counteract negative feelings they already have about themselves. Teachers must learn to send "I feel" mesages rather than "I expect" messages to avoid discouragement. For example, it's as easy to say, "I feel you are really concentrating today" as it is to say "I expect you to concentrate today," and the messages are entirely different. Learn to praise behavior rather than comment on the character of the child.

Planning additional ways to enhance the student's performance while providing opportunities to develop a good self-image can be successfully accomplished within the context of the classroom. For instance, students can be provided with situations that require that they make choices, which also provides them a chance to experience the consequences of their own decision-making. It is also important to assign academic tasks that the children can perform; for example, if some students read at a third-grade level, do not provide them with a sixth-grade text that will cause frustration and reinforce negative self-esteem. Another important strategy is to avoid activities in which a children's abilities will be compared with those of other students. In those situations, someone will always feel inferior. Deaf children become very used to failure and do not need to be set up by the teacher to fail again. You will soon notice that deaf children also become adept at avoiding failure by avoiding possible failure situations in and out of the classroom.

Effective teachers, then, provide opportunities for success for their students. They recognize that all children are individuals who learn at different rates. They make provisions for these individual differences within the classroom. It seems apparent that learning occurs most rapidly when the learner is successful at a task and receives positive reinforcement for learning.

Structuring the Classroom

Classrooms themselves can be structured to provide opportunities for successful learning. First of all, they must be pleasant, well organized, and comfortable for the students. Effective teachers are those who are highly sensitive to what is happening in their classrooms and who are able to head off trouble. This helps to make the classroom a safe place for the students. One way to achieve this is to decide in advance which behaviors are acceptable and which behaviors will not be allowed in the classroom. Some suggestions for establishing rules in the classroom are as follows:

1. Rules may be written, spoken, or signed, and should be stated positively. Why say "We don't run in the halls," when it is as easy to say "We walk in the halls,"? Why give students ideas by saying "We don't stick gum under our desks," when we can say "Gum goes from the mouth into the wastebasket,"?

2. Limit rules to those that are necessary. Too many rules can be depressing. Students may begin to feel they are in a jail instead of a classroom.

3. Always include a description of the positive effects of following a rule.

4. Involve students in the formation of classroom rules. If students are allowed to participate in the formation, they will be less likely to violate the rules.

5. Establish precisely what the expectations mean for each student.

6. If a rule seems to be too abstract or if the language level of the students is low, demonstrate exactly what is expected in terms of the rule. Demonstrations eliminate the opportunities for students to say they did not understand the rule.

7. Small misbehaviors can often be ignored. Occasional lapses can be expected to occur in any classroom at any time. If too much attention is paid to them, this provides negative reinforcement and negative reinforcement can become positive in the eyes of some students.

8. Finally, in upholding any rule, be consistent with the response. Unfair punishment or favoritism will be viewed with distrust by the students; this will encourage testing behaviors or direct challenges.

Effective teachers understand that modeling and imitation are important learning processes. Remember that negative modeling can be learned just as quickly as positive modeling and is very difficult to unlearn. Modeling suitable behavior is as important as modeling correct language in classrooms for the hearing-impaired.

Effective teachers are able to establish a good rapport with their students and are able to interact freely and easily with all members of the class. They constantly evaluate the kinds of information they are communicating to their students about their own feelings. The status of the teacher-child relationship must be monitored at all times as children are very sensitive to how they are perceived by their teacher. To be effective, teachers must establish well-defined performance expectations while maintaining an open and supportive relationship. A major consideration is the recognition that interpersonal relationships should reflect the language capabilities of the students. In order to show respect for students, communication should occur through the primary language system of each individual learner (speech, a signed English system, American Sign Language [ASL]).

Delivering Instruction

Effective teachers are able to communicate to their students exactly what it is the students are expected to learn. They are able to clearly inform students about *what* is to be done and *how* it is to be done. In addition to relieving anxiety, this will influence how students prepare for class and how they participate in the lessons. Information can be imparted through verbal instruction, written instruction, signed instructions, pictures, demonstration, or any combination, depending on the needs of the students in the classroom.

Clear goals affect how teachers prepare for and conduct their classes. Goals and objectives will not only be appropriate for the content but will also consider the level of the students. Long-term and short-term goals provide direction. In order to accomplish anything, we must first know where we are going and discover the best course for getting there. Specific terminal behaviors need to be set that consider language levels; they must take into consideration whether the class consists of college-bound, vocational-track, or self-sufficiency students.

Competent teachers know where to begin instruction by establishing entry levels that are designed to reduce student and teacher frustration. Teachers should properly pace instruction beginning with the simple and building toward mastery. This pace is defined by the conditions required to learn new behaviors and skills. Lessons should be sequenced from the simplest steps to the more difficult ones. This requires analyzing tasks into component skills and subskills. An effective teacher will never say "This is easy," because if some students do not understand it or get it wrong, they will feel stupid. To relieve anxiety, it is better to say "This may be tough," so when the children are successful, they feel inflated and competent. Learning is a permanent change which is observable and measurable. Good instruction is constantly being evaluated and constantly being adjusted. Evaluative measures need to be built into lesson plans. This is a critical component of the teaching and should be a part of the regular teaching process. Students and teachers receive prompt and relevant feedback with the right evaluation strategies. Ongoing assessment will indicate whether or not the materials and techniques being used are appropriate. New lesson plans and strategies can be planned using the results of the evaluation.

(More information on tests and using their results will be discussed in Chapter 4).

Classroom Management

Motivation! What is it and why is it important? What relationship does it have to classroom management? We have probably been told that, as educators, we should not expect learning to take place without motivation. It is considered to be the driving force behind learning. The dictionary defines *motivation* as "the incentive to act brought about by an internal or external stimulation." How do we, as teachers, instill this incentive or desire to learn?

In every classroom, there are always some students who seem to have a greater desire to learn than others. They are identified by their teachers as the "motivated" students. Motivation seems to be clearly tied to success or reward, which is accompanied by feelings of self-satisfaction. It is important to remember, as teachers of deaf children, that students' past experiences with failure have presented very few opportunities for them to feel good about themselves. Understandably, as a result of a history of failure, deaf students may be poorly motivated.

When confronted with unmotivated students, teachers also find themselves facing particular problems: communication becomes more difficult, discipline problems increase, anxiety is heightened in both the teacher and the students, and teaching becomes a chore. This leads to the burn-out syndrome, with teachers leaving the classroom for other careers. Unfortunately, teaching has never been a lucrative profession, so, ideally, teachers should at least enjoy what they are doing.

Why is it so difficult to motivate children in school? The major reason is probably because school happens almost daily. Day after day, week after week, children are expected to be high on learning. That high level of functioning is very difficult, if not impossible, for students and teachers to maintain. Anything that must be done daily quickly becomes ordinary and routine rather than an enjoyable experience.

How does motivation work in the classroom? First, let's talk about what does not motivate. Threats do not motivate, yet many teachers try to use them to motivate or control students. Threatening to call parents, to give lower grades, or to keep the students after school quickly loses its power. The main response that threatening teachers get from the students is resentment. Threats only serve to demean students and they imply that the students are not responsible for themselves while also advertising that the teacher is not able to maintain control of the class. In return for threats, students often respond with passive-aggressive behavior. For example, students may begin turning in sloppy or tardy work, or they may engage in distracting, negative behaviors, all of which lead to more teacher frustration, resulting in more threats. These new threats, of course, encourage more negative behavior on the childrens' part, which causes the teacher to give more threats, and on and on.

Motivation is an ambiguous, intangible concept that requires planning in order to be effective. According to Wlodkowski

(1984), every learning situation, regardless of length, is divided according to a time continuum: a beginning, a middle, and an end. During each phase, there is potential to employ motivational methods to influence and maximize learning. Let's examine these critical periods and motivational factors identified by Wlodkowski and relate them to us as teachers of deaf children.

1. *Beginning:* when the students enter and start the learning process.
   a. *Attitude:* the students' reactions to the general learning environment, the teacher, the subject matter, and their selves
   b. *Needs:* the requirements of students

2. *During:* when the students are involved in the learning process
   a. *Stimulation:* the process affecting the student
   b. *Affect:* the emotional experience of the student while learning

3. *Ending:* when the students are completing the learning process.
   a. *Competence:* the ability gained by the student as a result of learning
   b. *Reinforcement:* the value attached to the learning experience for the student

Phase 1: Beginning

As we have already seen, many deaf children come to self-contained schools or classes with little experience, language, or self-confidence. By the time they have had a couple years of failure and frustration in academic areas, most have developed a negative attitude about school in general or about specific content classes. Be aware of the history of your students. Establish a relationship with them so they learn to trust you. If your lessons consistently contain some recognizable value for the students and are not just busy work, your students will be more willing to participate and put forth the effort to complete their work. Listen to your students and learn about them, what interests them, what turns them off, etc. Accept their feelings, their fears, and their frustrations; these are real concerns for your students.

Phase 2: During

During the second phase, be aware of the climate of the classroom. A positive climate will facilitate student involvement, thus influencing motivation. Awareness of what is happening in the classroom will help avoid behavior problems and communication breakdowns. Mastery builds a sense of competence while failure decreases motivation. Motivate students by developing their self-esteem while building on student interests, which are, intrinsically, a significant source of motivation. A variety of opportunities should be provided that encourage the successful participation of all students in class. Remember that your students have a high level of need for achievement. Success is internally rewarding and is highly motivational in itself. Success will encourage students to participate willingly as well as help them to realistically assess their capabilities. Avoid high levels of competition with its inherent result: someone must lose. Finally, remember that providing an atmosphere of acceptance and caring does not mean you need to accept inappropriate behavior. Learn how to display rejection of unacceptable or harmful behaviors while still showing acceptance of the child. Acknowledge effort and reinforce completion of any lesson or activity.

Phase 3: Ending

At this point, it is important to help your students realize what has been learned. Acknowledge their responsibilities in completing the task. To provide closure, summarize with the students. In addition, allowing them to have input in determining their grades will provide clear evidence of future expectations as well as provide an avenue for smooth transition into the next activity.

Maslow's Hierarchy of Needs

Before any of the above can be effective, certain physiological needs must be met. A need can be considered a force that moves a person toward a goal. According to Maslow's theory of needs

(Maslow, 1968), unless basic requirements are met, learning becomes extremely difficult, if possible at all. For instance, a hungry, cold, or wet student will be involved internally with directing all energy and thought to coping with the deprivation felt at the time. Maslow wrote that self-actualization, knowing, and understanding and aesthetic needs can be met only after deficiency needs are met. You will need to become familiar enough with your students so you know immediately, as they enter your classroom, if particular students have specific needs to be met that day.

Physiological Needs

1. Be aware of room temperature. Children will not be able to work comfortably if they are too hot or too cold.

2. Do any of your students come to school hungry? Children cannot concentrate on academics if their stomachs are empty and growling.

3. Check noise level. Some of the students will be wearing hearing aids which amplify sounds. A common annoyance in the classroom is the buzzing noise that emanates from fluorescent lighting. This can cause pain to the child whose aid is designed to receive high-frequency sounds. Other common noises can also be distracting as well if they are not controlled.

4. Snow and rain are culprits too. If students arrive in the

classroom wet or cold from recess or walking to school, they will have to be dried off and warmed up before they will be ready to put any effort into school work.

5. Rest breaks should be incorporated into the daily schedule. This is especially important with younger children, but older students also need stretch breaks to eliminate boredom or to break lapses into daydreaming. Standing, stretching, and yawning will help the circulation while allowing the students to move around with the blessing of the teacher. Alert, awake students learn, bored and restless ones do not.

6. Remember that lipreading, reading signs, and finger-spelling take a great deal of effort and concentration, both mentally and visually. Whereas hearing children can look away from the teacher or other speakers, deaf children must continually focus on the speaker's face and hands. If another student is speaking, the children must turn, find the speaker, and turn back to the teacher at the appropriate time. Any loss of a word or sentence can seriously disrupt or distort the message. Can you imagine being expected to receive visually, process cognitively, comprehend, and carry out a two-sentence set of directions when for some reason or another you have blinked, rubbed your eye, or been momentarily distracted? It's imperative that as teachers of hearing-impaired students, we realize that receiving all information visually is physically taxing and mentally draining. Minimally, we should add a few additional minutes to the stretch break to allow students to rest their eyes.

All of the above should be considered when planning daily activities. A lesson that requires a great deal of visual and mental alertness might well be offered in the morning when students are fresh rather than during the afternoon.

Safety Needs

These needs reflect the basic security of individuals. Your commitment to the safety needs of your students will be found in the way you structure your classroom. Do you provide your students with a safe, secure place in the school environment? Are your lessons and expectations designed to give your students freedom from anxiety or danger? Is your classroom free from fear and threat to your pupils? Do not expect initiative and self-discipline from insecure students. Students want to feel comfortable and secure.

Ways to provide a safe atmosphere include the following:

1. A classroom that is secure is organized and orderly. This means you should establish clear rules for your classroom, and you should be able to show your pupils that you expect the rules to be followed. Maintain a sense of orderliness so students know where to find certain things that they will need during the day.

2. A safe classroom is predictable. This includes supporting students' expectations that you administrate your classroom rules fairly and consistently across all students. Insecurity results from not knowing how to act around a given topic or situation.

3. Never use ridicule or embarrassment in your classroom. Remember, you cannot scare or embarrass a child into wanting to learn. In fact, students who feel they may be subjected to such experiences will withdraw in order to avoid this type of interaction.

4. Watch for potential bullies. Every classroom seems to have a child who is able to overtly or covertly bully other children into doing his or her work, misbehaving, or acting in other unacceptable ways.

5. When appropriate, select projects or examples that are within the experience of the children to introduce or reinforce new concepts. This will eliminate a lot of guessing as well as eliminating the fear of making a mistake in front of others.

Need for Love and Belonging

As human beings, we all have an innate desire for affection and acceptance within a family or group. Students want to feel that they belong to the classroom and to become functional members of the class. If they do not, they will feel lonely, rejected, isolated, etc. To provide an accepting atmosphere within your classroom, be aware of the following:

1. Learn each student's name as quickly as possible. This will indicate to students that each one of them is an important addition to your class.

2. Learn the likes, dislikes, abilities, and weaknesses of your students and be sensitive to them when assigning duties or projects. By taking advantage of their interests, you will motivate the students while allowing them to feel you accept their preferences as worthwhile. It can be helpful to keep index cards that contain information specific to each child.

The Need for Esteem

We all feel the need to have self-respect and a sense of adequacy as a person. By having experiences that enable us to demonstrate our competencies or accomplishments, our concepts of ourselves as worthy persons increase. In your classroom, the following ideas will serve to promote your students' self-esteem:

1. Allow each student to participate in the decision-making processes that occur within your classroom. These can include such things as class projects or where to go on field trips. Solicit suggestions or ideas from students who seldom contribute to these decisions. This will provide these students an opportunity to feel their input is valuable and will enhance their feelings of self-worth.

2. Provide opportunities for students to express their feelings. This is often very difficult for deaf children. They need to learn to accept their feelings, which, in turn, will help them to learn about themselves. Accept the students' feelings and let

them know it's okay to have and express different emotions.

3. Double check all books and materials used in your classroom for cultural, sexual, or racial discrimination. Make every effort to ensure that only correct and positive racial, ethnic, and gender information is conveyed. Any material that portrays derogatory messages about a minority will adversely affect any child of that cultural background. Be sensitive to ethnic differences. Include materials in your classroom that reflect ethnic heros or holidays in a positive way. Your students have a right to have pride in who they are. This means you should include deaf heros as well (see Appendix B).

4. As teachers, we need to help students gain a realistic awareness of their strengths. This will allow them to develop an honest sense of personal effectiveness. Without this, deaf children learn dependency on teachers or parents. This dependency makes them prone to manipulation by others and can lead to a false sense of self. This leads to an overly dependent individual who is unable to make decisions, which in turn promotes a lowered self-concept.

5. To attain goals that affirm and enhance your students' identities, provide materials or assignments that complement their strengths and assets. This includes being aware of each student's capabilities, especially in reading, language, and communication skills. For example, self-esteem will not be enhanced by providing a 12-year-old deaf student with a second-grade reader even though this may be his or her actual reading level. You

will need to make a great effort to find or make materials that reflect students' ages as well as their academic functioning. We must avoid placing students in situations where they may be ridiculed or teased by others for having "baby books." Inappropriate materials and activities will result in inadequate motivation (see Appendix B for suggestions).

6. Offer subjects in a way that will encourage your students' independence as learners or people. You can do this by setting individual goals and providing ways to attain these goals. Allow each student the opportunity to participate in setting his or her own goals and determining strategies to achieve them.

7. Plan activities to allow students to display and share their work and talents. Remember, everyone is good at something. Arrange your classroom in a way that will provide students the chance to demonstrate their particular skills. An easy way is to plan bulletin boards to show off students' work. However, a word of caution is necessary here. Be sure not to make this display of work into a competitive situation—that is, avoid comparisons. Remember, in any competition, someone always loses. Too many losses will contribute to the development of a fatalistic attitude. Self-esteem will be poor and the student will stop trying.

Improving Self-Concept

Unless students feel self-confident or have good self-esteem, they will not be motivated to learn. Deaf children often come to school with very little self-confidence. This means that teachers must help them acquire feelings of achievement and success.

1. Children become used to being evaluated at every task. Teachers need to learn how to provide recognition and positive praise for correct responses during lessons or activities. Quick remarks such as "right," "good work," "you're really thinking," etc., provide encouragement and can have a greater effect on deaf children than withholding praise until the end.

2. Throw away your red pencils. Covering the students' paper, expecially papers of low-ability students, with red check marks will only serve to teach children they are incapable. Red check marks do not teach students their mistakes, they simply highlight and reinforce errors.

3. Avoid situations in which children will be compared with one another. Low-ability students cannot compete—they will always lose. Constantly being the last or lowest will only serve to encourage the students to stop even trying.

4. Make an effort to discover the specific skills or talents of your low ability students. It may be possible for them to excel in some nonacademic area. Encourage them to demonstrate their particular skills for their peers. Teacher and peer approval does much to promote a positive self-concept.

5. Provide low-functioning students with both public and private positive reinforcement for good academic work. It is important to shower praise and attention on such students for their successes. This may be the only positive reinforcement they get, and it may be all that prevents them from giving up in school.

6. Provide praise for effort as well as mastery. If you wait until mastery, some students may never receive positive feedback. A good concentrated effort may be the best the student is able to give.

7. Praise behavior rather than the character of the student. Instead of saying "You're a good boy," try to concentrate on what the student did. For example, "Thank you for picking up the papers, that really helped me."

8. Never, never tell students, that the lesson or activity is easy. If you do, and failure follows, the child will feel stupid or inadequate. Instead, if you say the lesson will be tough or difficult, self-image will be enhanced with success.

9. Be sure to emphasize the positive qualities of all students, especially your low functioning pupils, during parent conferences. Parents are usually well aware of their child's poor academic functioning, so there is no need to dwell on that aspect. Instead, mention any moments of academic or nonacademic success. In any educational environment, parents do not need to be reminded of their child's inadequacies.

10. Be aware of how you are perceived by your students. Both your verbal and nonverbal behaviors relate an image to each child. How your students see your perceptions of them is vitally important to their development.

Summary

One theme keeps presenting itself throughout this chapter. Success in the classroom for deaf children is very much a function of the skill of the teacher. A number of suggestions and strategies have been presented to guide teachers in their efforts to provide a classroom conducive to learning.

Deaf children, as a group as well as individuals, are unique learners. Therefore, their teachers must be equipped with skills to develop the kinds of programs that will enable deaf children to be successful students. Curricular concerns comprise one area of importance. Unless attending a residential school for the deaf that has its own curriculum designed specifically for deaf children, your students will be exposed to curriculum designed for hearing children. Based on your knowledge of the cognitive and language functioning of deaf children and their reading levels, you will need to adapt the curriculum before implementation. The communication skills and abilities of each child should be recognized and used in the classroom. This may involve using several modes in group instruction as well as individually.

In addition, effective teachers of the deaf must assume responsibility for motivating learners who have consistently experienced failure and frustration. This involves providing an environment in which the children can acquire feelings of achievement and self-worth. School may be the only place where some deaf children can find success. Materials, techniques of presentation, and classroom structure and management all contribute to building self-esteem and meeting students' needs.

Finally, it is important to remember that all children are individuals with different needs. Teachers therefore must be aware of each student's strengths and weaknesses and find out early what reinforces their growth.

CHAPTER
· 4 ·

Planning Lessons

*T*eaching deaf children is one of the most complex, demanding, yet satisfying experiences within the teaching profession. The skills and abilities needed to be successful in a classroom for the deaf are considerable. Not only must one love working with children on a daily basis, but one must also have the skills to read, interpret, and use psychological and academic assessment tools; understand the principles of developmental learning upon which curricula are built; be knowledgeable in the area of language development; understand the developmental stages of human cognition and memory; understand the learning and emotional problems that often accompany severe sensory deprivation; be an expert in the language and reading functioning of hearing-impaired students; have the ability to modify, adapt, and create teaching methods and materials to make them appropriate for the individual needs of deaf students; have the skills to teach content areas; have expertise in knowing how to evaluate learning; and be an effective classroom manager who provides a pleasant and motivating environment that builds positive attitudes and behaviors while it presents opportunities for learning.

There is no single approach to teaching deaf children. This chapter provides some techniques and considerations for planning lessons, however, while considering the above mentioned areas of concern (see Figure 4–1).

The initial step in planning lessons requires identification of exactly what it is you want to teach. You must first establish what skills are to be mastered by your students and/or what concepts you expect them to acquire.

Your topic and the depth in which you'll examine it will determine the length of your unit, the materials used, your procedures, the activities to be included, and how you will evaluate what learning has taken place. In order to be effective, each step must be planned prior to instruction.

Identification of What You Will Teach

By carefully identifying and clarifying target skills or concepts, inappropriate or superfluous content will be eliminated while essential content will be retained. Having identified the skills or concepts to be taught, your next step is to establish long-term goals and short-term objectives.

In doing this, the time element must be given consideration. You must decide what learning your students will achieve

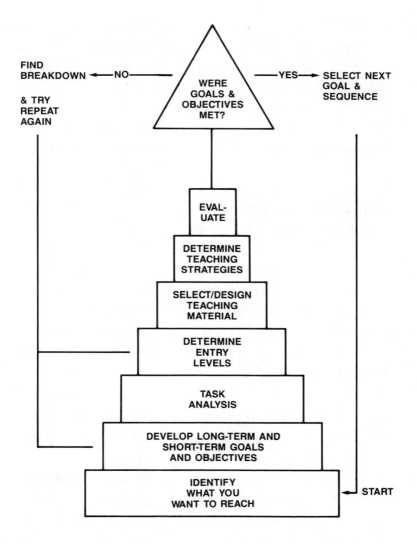

FIND
BREAKDOWN ◄──NO──── WERE ──YES──► SELECT NEXT
GOALS & GOAL &
& TRY OBJECTIVES SEQUENCE
REPEAT MET?
AGAIN

EVAL-
UATE

DETERMINE
TEACHING
STRATEGIES

SELECT/DESIGN
TEACHING
MATERIAL

DETERMINE
ENTRY
LEVELS

TASK
ANALYSIS

DEVELOP LONG-TERM AND
SHORT-TERM GOALS
AND OBJECTIVES

IDENTIFY
WHAT YOU ◄── START
WANT TO REACH

by the end of a given period of time. Some topics or content will require only a short period of time to be accomplished while others must be carried over longer periods of time. For example, specific and concrete concepts (e.g., math facts such as 2 + 2 = 4) will be easily acquired in a relatively short period of time while attitude or behavior changes (e.g., on-the-job behavior) will require a considerably longer time to accomplish.

Long-Range Goals and Short-Term Objectives

Long-range goals are generally described in broad terms and define or describe desired terminal behaviors. Attainable long-range goals will provide the basis for your lessons. They can be simple, complex, individual, or group goals. In contrast, instructional objectives are short-term, day-to-day behaviors designed for incremental learning; each accomplished objective will bring the students closer to the specified long-term goals. Accomplished objectives are visible displays by the learners that demonstrate successful completion of lesson objectives along with the degree of success.

Behaviorally written instructional objectives require clear statements that include (1) the behaviors to be observed, (2) the conditions under which these behaviors will occur, and (3) clear performance criteria by which to judge acceptability of performance. Behavioral objectives must state how accurately, rapidly, or frequently a specified behavior is to occur. Through criteria, you can monitor the students' progress toward the long-term goals. Learning is observable and measurable and will be evident in the students' performance or change in their behaviors. Behavior that can't be shown can't be assumed to have been learned; therefore, your objectives must clearly describe the behavior students are to exhibit in order to demonstrate mastery of a task. It is also important to be realistic in setting goals.

Example 1

Long-Range Goal

To learn that fruits and vegetables and other plants come from seeds.

Short-Range Behavioral Objectives

Given different kinds of seeds, the children will be able to match them with the fruit they come from with 80 percent accuracy.

Given the identified seeds, the children will be able to classify them according to size, and as to whether or not we eat the seeds themselves, with 90 percent accuracy.

Example 2

Long-Range Goal

To learn more about fractions.

Short-Range Behavioral Objectives

Given two equivalent fractions, the student will correctly write the numbers used to multiply to obtain the equivalency nine out of ten times.

Given one fraction and the number used to multiply to find an equivalent fraction, the student will correctly compute the new equivalent fraction nine out of ten times.

Given one fraction and the denominator of a potentially equivalent fraction, the student will write the correct numerator to make the two fractions equivalent eight out of ten times.

Example 3

Long-Range Goal

To be able to produce a well-organized, coherent outline for writing a report or giving a speech.

Short-Range Behavioral Objectives

Given a group of paragraphs, the student will produce an outline of the paragraphs, correctly choosing the ideas to use as main topics, subtopics, and details. This task will be repeated until it is 100 percent correct.

Given previous instruction, the student will use his or her own notes as a guide for outline construction. This will be done as needed for each student to achieve 90 percent accuracy.

Task Analysis

In addition to identifying a goal, you need to know what is required for the learner to achieve the goal. Therefore, once your objectives have been formulated, you will need to analyze them systematically—that is, you will need to break down the steps or skills required to achieve the terminal behavior into a hierarchy of prerequisites. You must be able to identify what students need to know at each step and correctly sequence these steps into teachable components. Unfortunately, the steps are not always obvious. Therefore, you must ask yourself these questions:

1. What must each student do in order to reach the desired goal?

2. Is there a logical order of learning to achieve these tasks?

3. What skills or knowledge are needed to achieve each step?

The breaking down into systematically ordered prerequisites for any given task is called *task analysis*. Task descriptions are valuable tools for understanding exactly what is involved to complete each objective and to properly sequence instruction. The easiest way to do task analysis is to first describe your behavioral objective and then work backward one step at a time until you have identified all the necessary prerequisites.

Example 1

Behavioral Objective

Given 20 addition problems containing four-digit numbers with regrouping, the child will be able to calculate the sums of 18 out of the 20 problems.

Prerequisite Knowledge

14. Can add three-digit numbers requiring regrouping of ones, tens, and hundreds

13. Can add three-digit numbers requiring regrouping of ones and tens.

12. Can add three-digit numbers requiring regrouping of ones

11. Can add three-digit numbers without regrouping

10. Can add two-digit numbers requiring regrouping of ones and tens

9. Can add two-digit numbers requiring regrouping of tens

8. Can add two-digit numbers requiring regrouping of ones

7. Can add two-digit numbers without regrouping

6. Knows addition properties of order and zero

5. Can calculate sums 11 to 18

4. Can calculate sums 6 to 10

3. Can calculate sums 0 to 5

2. Knows addition terms

1. Knows the meaning of addition

Example 2

Behavioral Objective

When asked to tell what time it is, the student will correctly state the time to the minute, with 90 percent accuracy.

Prerequisite Knowledge

11. Can tell time to 5 minutes

10. Can tell time to the quarter hour

9. Can tell time to the half hour

8. Can tell time to the hour

7. Knows what the minute hand does

6. Knows what the hour hand does

5. Knows which way the clock hands move

4. Can count to 55 by multiples of 5

3. Can count by quarter and half hours

2. Can count by ones to 60

1. Knows what a clock is

Example 3

Behavioral Objective

Given first-grade lined paper and asked to write the alphabet, the students will be able to write from Aa to Zz correctly and legibly with 90 percent accuracy.

Prerequisite Knowledge

7. Can write the letters of the alphabet

6. Can trace the letters of the alphabet

5. Can name the letters of the alphabet

4. Can match uppercase letter with corresponding lower-case letter

3. Can put alphabet letters in order

2. Can recite alphabet in order

1. Knows what a letter is

Determining Entry Levels

One of the values of task analysis is that the teacher can identify the appropriate starting place in any specific task for each individual student, depending on his or her previous experience and knowledge of the task. The entry level of students is ascertained by finding out what they know about the specific subject as well as the level of present performance. The prerequisites generated by task analysis and knowledge of each student's entry level provide your instructional starting point. This is important in terms of encouraging positive attitudes in the students in the learning situation. The ideal is to find the readiness level for learning new tasks for each student. This will help prevent discipline problems that can arise when a student is bored by material already mastered or frustrated by material that is too difficult.

One way to determine a student's entry level is to use a pretest developed from the prerequisites generated by your task analysis for any particular objective.

Factors That Influence Learning

Due to the learning and emotional difficulties imposed by severe hearing impairments, you will want to examine the students' records in order to understand their individual needs as fully as possible. Student characteristics and learning facts will influence learning and motivation and thus affect your teaching plans. To determine students' instructional needs you will want to obtain information regarding the following:

1. Psychological assessment

2. Academic functioning

3. Classroom behavior

4. Language skills

5. Medical history

The psychological assessment is not to be read to determine IQ or learning quotient, rather to analyze scores on each subtest. By doing this, you will find practical information about your students' strengths and weaknesses and about sensorimotor problems that may interfere with learning. Subtest scores will reveal the coding, discrimination, visual-motor, visual-tracking, and short-term and long-term memory functioning of each student, which will be valuable in setting up an effective instructional plan (see Chapter 3). This is important information as you will want to focus on your students' strengths while remediating weak areas. This will also help you identify where a student may break down in the learning process.

Scores on measures of academic functioning will provide information regarding academic achievement and competency. As with the psychological reports, you will not use the results to place limits on the potential for achievement, but rather as vehicles for determining aptitude. The profile of both psychological and academic tests will help identify where a student's main difficulties lie and help define instructional priorities. This information will aid in planning the rate of input, the amount of input, and the sequence of instruction.

Information on classroom behavior will also be available in student records or through reports by previous teachers and will be substantiated or refuted by your observations. You will want to know if behaviors exhibited by your student are goal-directed: Are there testing, controlling, or manipulative behaviors that are characteristic of certain students? Your main purpose for looking at behavioral records is to look for specific behaviors that are manifested during particular activities. Are hyperactive or avoidance behaviors evident consistently during specific tasks? Do certain student combinations set the stage for conflict? After all, students are human and have different personality characteristics that interact positively or negatively with others in their environment. You will want to avoid pairing certain students for class assignments if that pairing will result in disruptive behaviors.

When looking at language skills, be aware of the mode used most effectively by the student (i.e., signing, speech, speech-reading, reading, writing, etc.). You will want to teach to the strongest mode. Additionally, you will need to look at both recep-tive and expressive skills. You will also want to distinguish between linguistic competency and communicative ability. You may need to provide oral tests in order to adequately assess what your students know. To be effective, you must allow each student to use his or her intact language skills.

Medical records will provide information on any drugs your students are taking. You'll want to be aware of any side effects of the medication as well as the time of day it is taken. Drowsiness and fatigue factors can influence the ability to concentrate and may thereby cause you to alter your schedule to accomodate these reactions to certain drugs. Teachers spend so much time with students that they are often in the position to question the cor-rectness or amount of specific medications for particular students. Beside medication, information regarding certain afflictions is available (e.g., seizures). By knowing what to look for, teachers can often tell when a seizure is coming on and can prepare for it.

Materials for Teaching

The materials used in presenting or reinforcing concepts taught will be determined by what is available and what you are able to create. Usually only portions of commercially prepared materials and texts are appropriate for deaf children with their reading and language deficits. However, don't dismiss them com-pletely, as they can be useful tools in terms of ideas, references, structure, and sequence.

Select material that is easily adaptable as you will need to modify and rewrite it to ensure and enhance comprehension in your students (see Appendix A). To *adapt* means to make adjustments so that the material fits a specified use. You adapt curricula any time you make changes to make them appropriate for deaf children. Adaptation can include restructuring, resequencing, eliminating unnecessary content, or adding content to commercially prepared materials.

Here is a sample paragraph:

> Some dinosaurs had scaly skins. How do we know this, since bones and teeth are all that remain of their bodies? Sometimes dinosaurs left skin prints where thay had been lying in sand. The sand slowly turned to sandstone. Now, millions of years later, scientists can see the prints and know that the beasts were scaly. (Branley, 1974)

There are a number of possible changes to make the material less difficult or extreme. A *modified* paragraph would be as follows:

Example 1

> Some dinosaurs had scaly skins. How do we know this, when bones and teeth are all that are left of their bodies? Sometimes dinosaurs left marks from their skin where they had been lying in the sand. The sand slowly turned into rock. Now, many many years later, scientists can see the marks in the rock and know that the dinosaurs were scaly.

A rewritten paragraph, on the other hand, would be changed more extensively:

Example 2

> All that is left of the dinosaurs' bodies are bones and teeth. But we still know that dinosaurs had scaly skins. We know this because sometimes dinosaurs left skin prints where they had been lying in sand. The sand slowly turned into sandstone. Now it is millions of years later and scientists can tell the dinosaurs were scaly from the skin prints in the sand.

There may not be anything available that suits your needs, so you will be forced to spend considerable effort and many hours developing instructional or supplemental materials. Your materials are important as they provide substance for what is taught; therefore, they should be motivating, of high interest, and manipulative. Be creative—novelty sparks interest in students. Use a multisensory, multimedia approach to present new information. Transparencies, pictures, posters, models, diagrams, charts, graphs, etc, are available or can easily be made and all lend themselves to providing visual, concrete support for linguistic or abstract concepts. Four fundamental concerns should direct your selection and preparation of materials.

Language Difficulty

This will be the most obvious factor you encounter with hearing-impaired students. In your evaluation of materials and texts for your students, you must evaluate the language content first. In controlling the language, take into consideration the theory that language develops and progresses from the simple to complex. The frustration experienced and acted out by deaf children in classrooms is often the direct result of their inability to comprehend material due to the language presented. Variables you will want to look at include vocabulary, the number of complex sentences, the number of dependent clauses, multiple meanings, idiomatic and colloquial expressions, inflectional endings, and level of abstraction.

Age-Appropriateness

Lesson material must be age appropriate. Typically, due to the linguistic deficits of deaf children, commercial products that match their language abilities are too babyish in content and style. To burden your students with this material will reinforce the negative self-concepts already held by them. Instead, your adapted material should reflect the students' linguistic abilities and, at the same time, their personal interests. Find out what is important to them—cars, rockets, clothes, sports, TV stars, dating. . . .

Cognitive Levels

A third consideration in material selection is the cognitive level of your students. Cognition involves how a student thinks, organizes information, and generally integrates all levels of learning. There are three main conceptual levels: concrete, functional, and abstract.

Although your students may all be within the same chronological age range, you should expect to find great individual differences in their cognitive and symbolic abilities. As discussed in Chapter 2, most studies on the cognitive development of deaf children indicate that they generally exhibit late development in logical thinking or concrete operations and symbolic or formal operations. Typically they lag 1 to 3 years behind hearing children with the lag becoming more noticeable as the children grow older. Therefore, materials designed for a 9-year-old hearing child would probably not be appropriate for a 9-year-old deaf child. For example, third-grade hearing children have large numbers of story problems in arithmetic. Word problems can be very complex, and, while a deaf child may have the computational skill to solve the problem, he or she may not have the linguistic competency to understand what the problem is asking.

Example 3

John has 7¢. His sister Mary has 3¢ more than John. How much money do they have together?

The most common response by deaf children would be to add 7¢ and 3¢. "More than" is a difficult concept and is often confusing. It is important to note that this word problem requires two mental tasks before it can be answered correctly. A visual representation along with the story problem would enhance the chances of the problem being solved correctly; also, the opportunity to demonstrate or reinforce the concept would be provided.

Example 4

On the back of a package containing sweet pea seeds, the directions stated, "Plant in soil 2 inches deep and 1 inch apart." Can you picture several little 2-inch piles of soil, 1 inch apart with one solitary sweet pea seed placed on top of each? These directions must be clarified to save the student from embarrassment.

In material selection, then, you must not only be aware of the differences between the cognitive functioning of hearing and deaf children, but you must also recognize differences among the children in your own class. Again, it is important to individualize instruction as much as possible. Effective instruction will provide hands-on, manipulative experiences for younger preoperational children, and it will include pictorial or other representational material to emphasize symbols for older, more cognitively advanced students. Written words are symbolic and require higher functioning cognitive ability. In rewriting material, it is important to avoid ambiguities and complex sentence structures unless that is what you are teaching.

Physical/Sensory Abilities

The fourth consideration in preparing materials for teaching is the physical/sensory abilities of your students. Be aware of motor problems or sensory limitations in addition to the degree and type of hearing loss. For example, due to visual deficiencies, some students will require print size to be larger than usual, or they may demonstrate problems reading at a distance (e.g., boardwork, overhead transparencies, etc.). Some students may exhibit sensory overload in the visual modality, and you will need to eliminate unnecessary visual information in the materials.

Summary

In order to be an effective teacher, you must plan thoroughly. First, you must identify exactly what it is you wish to teach. Then you must establish both long-range goals (desired terminal behaviors) and short-term objectives (day-to-day behaviors to bring learners closer to specified long-term goals). You will need to be able to task analyze each objective to understand the sequential steps required to achieve it. This will allow you to correctly sequence instruction and determine the entry level into each task for your individual students.

Your instruction will be affected by all factors that influence learning, including your students' skills and abilities, their strengths and weaknesses, their classroom behaviors, their communication modes, and their medical concerns.

Your teaching materials should provide substance for what is being taught. They should be multisensory and motivating, providing visual, concrete support for linguistic or abstract concepts. Four fundamental concerns should guide your selection: language-appropriateness, age-appropriateness, your students' cognitive levels, and your students' physical/sensory abilities.

Understanding
Test Information

*I*t is necessary to be aware of the present level of functioning of your students before developing teaching strategies. Your method of instruction, the abstractness of material, and decisions about group size and communication modes will vary depending on what you understand about the cognitive levels, the degrees of hearing loss, and the personal characteristics and academic skills of your students. This knowledge is easily obtained through records of standardized tests and teacher-made assessment tools. Results from good tests and other evaluative measures will provide the foundation for making sound instructional decisions.

Degree of Hearing Loss and Its Relationship to Learning

The degree of hearing loss will effect an individual's ability to understand speech and language. Although production and responses will vary with each student, Table 5–1 provides a general guideline for degrees of losses and expected consequences. This information is important when planning and implementing any academic activity.

Understanding Test Information

A primary concern in using standardized tests with hearing-impaired children is to understand exactly what the tests measure. The first consideration is the unique language and communication problems inherent in testing this specific population. One researcher, Conrad (1979) suggested that by school age, even hard-of-hearing children may have sustained enough neurological deficit to impair utilization of linguistic information received exclusively through auditory pathways.

Brill (1977), a long-time educator of the deaf, wrote that any test that involves language, either in its administration or in requiring the subject to respond verbally, is unfair because lack of language is the main handicap of the hearing impaired. Levine (1974) made a crucial point regarding verbal directions when administering any test to a deaf child: if the test directions are not comprehensible to the subject, the subject cannot

TABLE 5-1.

Degree of Hearing Loss and its Effects if Present From Birth

Degree of Loss	Effect of Loss on Understanding Speech and Language
Mild	May have problems hearing faint speech at a distance—will miss a fair amount of auditory information
20–30 db	Will probably "get along" in a regular classroom
	Will have good articulation
Marginal	Should be able to understand conversational speech at a distance of about 3 feet without a hearing aid
31–40 db	Will be able to carry on face-to-face conversation
	May miss as much as 50 percent of class discussion if voices are faint or not in line of vision
	Will require preferential seating, including the ability to move around when class activities change
	May display some speech production problems if loss is of the high-frequency type: difficulty will be with *s, z, sh, ch,* and *j*; substitution of *t* for *d, k* for *g*
	May display a limited vocabulary
	Will probably benefit from speech-reading training to learn how to use the visual input received
Moderate	Can understand loud conversation at about 3 feet and without hearing aids

(continued)

TABLE 5-1. (*continued*)

Degree of Loss	Effect of Loss on Understanding Speech and Language
41–55 db	Misunderstands unwittingly Delayed language development (will follow normal sequence) Normal voice—still able to monitor to some extent Will probably have defective speech Definitely needs hearing aids and visual (speech-reading) cues
Moderately severe 56–70 db	May hear moderate voice level several inches from ear (normal speech, 50–65 db) without hearing aids Will hear loud noises at some distance (car horn, dogs barking, very loud speech) without hearing aids Speech and language do not develop spontaneously unless aided from early childhood Voice quality still may be good May be able to discriminate between vowels but not all consonants Vision used as a support but aided audition should still be the primary means of input
Severe 71–90 db	Responds only to loud speech at a very close range without hearing aids Normal conversation not heard without amplification (even with amplification, some high-frequency–low-intensity consonants will not be heard) May function as deaf or hard-of-hearing (factors that seem to make the difference include presence or absence of early

Degree of Loss	Effect of Loss on Understanding Speech and Language
71–90 db (continued)	intervention, appropriate amplification, type of educational intervention, and amount and type of parent support
Profound	Auditory reception of voice may range from loud shout about 1 inch from ear to no response at all without hearing aids
91–95 db	May function as hard-of-hearing if above factors operate from infancy
95 db+	Unaware of loud noise although may react reflexively to loud sounds close to ear
	Speech and language do not develop spontaneously
	Audition is not the primary mode for language and speech reception; the visual channel is used for learning
	Amplification and/or other devices such as tactile aids used to perceive environmental sounds

Adapted from Streng, A., Fitch, W., Hedgecock, L., Phillips, J., & Carrell, J. (1958). *Hearing Therapy for children.* New York: Grune & Stratton, Inc.

do justice to him- or herself in carrying out the given task. In such instances, the test directions themselves become a test, which is not the intent of the procedure. Therefore, to be fair, test language must be modified to take the deaf students' needs into account. In other words, it is necessary to present the test in a mode of communication that is readily understood by the subject. Jensema (1975; 1980) suggested several ways this can be done, including simplifying the language, repeating, explaining, and using multiple communication modes. These, of course, deviate from the required procedures; hence, the next question is, Will the test still do what it is supposed to do? Also, how will the deviations from the established procedures affect the reliability and validity of the test?

Another concern involves the use of the language in multiple-choice achievement test items. Language must be con-trolled so as not to be more complex than is necessary to test an individuals knowledge of the subject being tested. Language complexity above what is minimally required could be consid-ered a verbal overload, thereby becoming a source of bias against people whose verbal skills are limited.

Vernon (1978) wrote that the deaf not only exhibit different language levels but that comprehension ability also appears to differ. This factor is complicated by varying skills in lipreading and manual communication. This means that in group testing situations, directions may have to be presented very carefully to allow each child present to understand fully and exactly what is expected of him or her. This could include any or all of the modifications mentioned earlier, plus it might be necessary to include different sign systems and/or pantomime.

Tomlinson-Keasey and Kelly (1974) presented an interesting idea concerning the testing of deaf children. It is based on a hypothesized hemispherical-lateralization difference and possi-ble differences in perceptual organization as a result of deaf students relying almost exclusively on visual input. Thus, deaf children are presumed to process language in the right hemi-sphere (or they may lack hemispheric specialization), since their input is visual; hearing children, on the other hand, process language in the left hemisphere due to auditory input. This information would lead to the conclusion that those tests that require higher levels of language symbolization and conceptualization would present problems to the hearing-impaired child. However, hearing-impaired students should also be more proficient on tasks requiring visual processing since these processes are presumed to be localized in the right hemisphere.

Moores (1978a) suggested that where the deaf have demonstrated inferior performances on tests, there is a very real possibility that the experimenters were unable to communicate effectively with the subjects. According to Levine (1974), differences on intelligence or achievement tests may be the direct result of experiential deprivation, including linguistic experience. Regardless of which reasoning is correct, the net effect is the same. Deaf students score consistently lower on IQ and achievement tests.

The Tests Themselves

Beside the issue of language, the tests themselves should be considered. Most tests *can* be given to hearing-impaired individuals, but doesn't that mean they *should* be.

The questions of validity and reliability of a test must be considered. A *reliable* test is one that yields similar scores for individuals after repeated administrations, over time. *Validity* is the degree to which a test actually measures what it purports to measure. A valid test must be a reliable test, but the reverse is not true.

Another consideration concerns the assumption that an individual with whom the test is used has been exposed to comparable learning experiences or acculturation as the original norming group. This point addresses itself directly to the issue of test bias. A test can only be considered valid in relationship to a particular group of individuals. What may be valid for one group may not be valid for a different group. The idea of test bias has been the source of much discussion and litigation, resulting in certain mandates concerning the rights of all handicapped children. Thus, information about cultural and social background must be considered when making test decisions, particularly in selecting standardized tests, for handicapped children. Hearing-impaired children must be given these same considerations. Hearing-impaired people, as a group, have not had the same opportunities to acquire language skills as hearing people; therefore, it is not fair to compare their performances.

IQ Tests

Several studies have shown that the Wechsler Intelligence Scales for Children (WISC) and the Wechsler Adult Intelligence Scales (WAIS) are the most popular and most often used assessment instruments for deaf persons (Levine, 1974). The WISC has provided norms for the deaf, but it has not been standardized on deaf children. The norms were established by obtaining test protocols of deaf children, identifying a "profile," and reassigning norm numbers. It is important to remember that the administration of the test was not standardized. The WISC-R (revised) is comprised of two scales: a verbal scale and a performance scale. Each contains six subtests. The verbal scale contains a set of verbal questions to which the examinee must respond verbally, and the performance scale involves various manipulation tasks. Most often, only the performance section of the WISC-R will be given to a hearing-impaired child. It is important to remember that the directions are given orally and that two of the performance subtests (picture arrangement and coding) have been shown to rely heavily on verbal mediation, which means that these two subtests are really testing the conceptual underpinnings of language.

Although the performance scale may provide a truer picture of a deaf child's ability, it is often advisable to note the verbal scale score, especially if the hearing-impaired child is being considered for placement in a regular hearing classroom. This scale assesses the child's ability to compete verbally with his or her hearing peers.

It has been shown that a discrepancy of 16 to 44 points can occur between performance and verbal scores. The discrepancy is usually greater for congenitally deaf students than for hard-of-hearing or postlingually deafened students.

It is important to break down the subtests in order to determine exactly what skill each subtest is measuring. Then, after examining the description of each subtest, we can develop a profile of the strengths and weaknesses of each student. The low areas will then be targeted as areas to be remediated while the areas with high scores can be used in our lessons to provide successful experiences.

Verbal Scale

1. *Information*. This measures general knowledge drawn from the environment. It involves rote long-term memory and reflects school-influenced education. It is culturally biased. A low score may be caused by any of the following:
    a. Hearing loss that restricts incidental learning
    b. Limited experience
    c. Mental retardation
    d. Cultural learning

2. *Comprehension*. This measures the ability to make judgments and everyday, practical understanding. It includes awareness of social customs and mores. A low score may be due to any of the following:
    a. Limited experience
    b. Poor judgment
    c. Inability to understand cause and effect relationships
    d. Impulsiveness

3. *Arithmetic*. This measures attention and concentration, numerical reasoning, application of basic arithmetic

skills, and the ability to use abstract concepts. A low score could reveal either or both of the following:

a. Inability to attend or concentrate for periods of time

b. Difficulty handling abstract concepts

4. *Similarities*. This measures the ability to handle verbal abstractions, to think in abstract concepts, and to do associative or divergent thinking. Low scores may be caused by the following:

a. Hearing loss and its effect on verbal skill development (i.e., limited vocabulary)

b. Concreteness

c. Perseveration

5. *Vocabulary*. This measures the ability to define words and the ability to use verbal information to reorganize ideas. Vocabulary scores are traditionally correlated with IQ scores. Low scores may be due to the following:

a. Hearing loss

b. Limited educational opportunities or achievement

c. Culturally disadvantaged environment

6. *Digit Span*. This measures rote memory and auditory recall, short-term memory, correlated symbols, and attention. Low scores may reveal the following:

a. Poor short-term memory

b. Impaired attention span

c. Anxiety and intolerance for stress

Performance Scale

1. *Picture Completion*. This measures the ability to visualize essential and nonessential detail and the judging of relationships. It also measures long-term memory, concentration, degree of persistence, and the ability to note missing details.

2. *Picture Arrangement*. This measures visual perception, sequentialization, and the ability to synthesize parts into a coherent whole. It also measures social intelligence and the ability to plan and adjust to new situations.

3. *Block Design*. This measures the ability to analyze and synthesize perceptional information. It involves logical reasoning as applied to space relations, along with visual-motor skills, nonverbal concept formation, and ability to handle failure. It also examines if attempts to complete a task are systematic or trial-and-error.

5. *Object Assembly*. This measures visual-motor organization and coordination along with the ability to reorganize patterns and synthesize parts into wholes. It also involves concrete nonverbal problem-solving and reveals the subject's thinking and working habits as well as his or her ability to handle ambiguity and persistence.

6. *Coding*. This measures psychomotor speed, visual-motor coordination, and the ability to learn new material in associative contexts. It also examines the subject's ability to persist at a task that requires continued concentration and effort.

Other IQ Tests Used With Hearing Impaired Students

The Hiskey-Nebraska Test of Learning Aptitude is often used with the deaf; it is the only test of intelligence designed specifically for use with hearing-impaired children (Mira, 1962). Designed to be used with children 3 through 16 years of age, the Hiskey-Nebraska has two sets of norms and two sets of directions: oral for hearing persons and pantomime for the deaf. It contains 12 subtests, half of which are memory tests (which again brings up the question of verbal mediation). The test provides age norms for the deaf, called "learning ages." The following tasks form the subtest skills in the Hiskey-Nebraska:

Bead Pattern

Memory For Color

Picture Identification

Picture Association

Paper Folding

Visual Attention Span

Block Patterns

Completion of Drawings

Memory For Digits

Puzzle Blocks

Picture Analogies

Spatial Reasoning

The Leiter International Point Performance Scale is another intelligence test used with the deaf (Levine, 1974; Mira, 1962). The Arthur adaptation of this test has pantomime directions and is appropriate only for children 2 to 12 years old. The Leiter was designed to be used with persons with speech and language difficulties and was standardized on a hearing population. The Leiter does not contain any subtests but is comprised of a series of unrelated tasks. The major caution with this test deals with determining exactly what the number score means. First, it is important to remember that the mean (the average score) on the Leiter is 95 as compared with every other test where the mean score is 100. Second, the tasks themselves have age norm "gaps." That is, a certain task may have age scores for the task at 2-0 and 3-0 and then none until 5-0. What is the appropriate score for a child who passes at the 2-0 and 3-0 levels but fails to pass the item at the 5-0 level?

Achievement Tests

The second type of formal testing we need to examine is the achievement test. The achievement test most often used with hearing impaired students is the Stanford Achievement Test-Hearing Impaired Form (SAT-HI).

The SAT was first published in 1923. It consists of a collection of six achievement test batteries with several subtests to assess skills in reading comprehension, math concepts, math computation, science, and social studies.

In 1972, a national survey was conducted by the Office of Demographic Studies (ODS) which showed that the SAT was the most popular standardized test among educators of the deaf. Of 29,023 hearing-impaired students to receive any standardized test during the 1972 to 1973 school year, approximately 77 percent or 22,292 took the SAT. Because of the obvious popularity of the SAT, the ODS decided to facilitate proper use by compiling a special edition: the SAT-HI.

There is still a great deal of misunderstanding and misinterpretation in regard to the scores of deaf children on the SAT-HI. The score of a deaf child does not mean the same as the score for a hearing child. A fourth-grade-level score in reading does not mean that the deaf child can read textbooks at a fourth-grade level or understand the same kind of material that the hearing child does who obtains an identical score (Brill, 1977). The basic reason for this is that there is only a limited number of questions that can be asked on any standardized test. Brill wrote that the correct answers a hearing child gives may represent a very small sample of that child's total language. On the other hand, a deaf child's correct answers on a standardized test may represent a high percentage of this child's total language.

Second, parallel forms of tests are given in order to avoid giving the same test twice to the same person. Again, Brill offered a caution. If a child is tested with form A and then retested with form B, ideally his or her scores should be nearly identical; however, this has proven unreliable with deaf children. Their scores may vary by 2 or 3 years when tested on two successive days with parallel forms of the same test. Consequently, if one form of the test is given at the beginning of a learning period and a parallel form given at the end, the difference in the scores will not reflect a true measure of the child's learning.

Examples of why this happens were offered by Brill, who referred to the language handicap of deaf children. For example, if one form of the test used the word *pail* and the parallel form used the word *bucket*, the two terms would probably be equivalent to a hearing child but not to a deaf child. Another example concerns question forms. The question, "What kind of _____?" is no harder for a hearing child than "What did _____ do?" However, unless a deaf child had been drilled on the question form, "What kind of _____?" he or she would probably have a great deal of trouble distinguishing between the more familiar adjectival form of the word *kind* (i.e., affectionate) and its less familiar use as a noun in question form. A third example: Hearing children have probably heard of Egypt and the Nile River long before they study about them in geography, but chances are the deaf child knows nothing about the Nile until seeing its name in print in geography class in seventh or eighth grade. Therefore, on a reading test, a paragraph about the Nile River may mean something to a hearing child where it may mean nothing at all to a deaf child.

Item wording is also important to consider; the wording may be such that the wrong skills are gauged. For example, although an item may be designed to gauge math abilities, that item may actually be assessing reading ability if it is difficultly worded. This is a major problem when tests are used with other minority children as well as with the hearing-impaired.

Brill offered other precautions related to the interpretation and use of test scores at extreme ends of the scale. At the lower end, where scores for second- and third-grade levels are interpreted, one, two, or three questions may make the difference of a grade score of as much as half a year. The likelihood of getting a correct answer by chance on such a small number of questions will invalidate most scores in the second- and third-grade range (Rudner, 1978). At the other end of the scale, the SAT is standardized only on children up to the ninth-grade level. There are scores for the 10th; 11th; and 12th-grade levels, but these are estimated scores; as such, they are even more invalid for deaf students.

The SAT was designed for public school children based on existing curricula in each grade in elementary schools. After items were selected for the test, norms, such as grade equivalent scores and percentiles, were developed. These norms provide a means for comparing the performance of one student or group of a students with that of some particular reference group. It must be remembered that in the revision of the SAT-HI, the test item wording was not changed, nor were the tables used in converting raw scores to grade scores adjusted. The ODS simply provided a pretest to be used with deaf children in order to determine at which level each particular child should be tested in each subject area. This means that one child could take a social studies test designed for primary level children, a reading test designed for intermediate children, and an arithmetic computation test for advanced children (Brill, 1977).

A major problem remains that the test, pretest, and battery comprise, in the strictest sense, a reading test. Even at the primary level, answers are printed so the child must read or choose the answer from reading the finger-spelling of the presenter. For example, in the primary battery vocabulary test, the words, "Food is cooked in the _____," are signed, while the possible answers are finger-spelled: parlor, den, kitchen. Hence, this section becomes a test of visual perception and short-term memory, not a strict vocabulary test. (Imagine saying to a hearing youngster, "Go get your f-i-r-e-t-r-u-c-k and I'll play with you"!) In the same manner, at the upper elementary level, all the social studies and science tests are comprised of reading paragraphs and responding to written questions. This puts hearing-impaired pupils at a disadvantage. Although they may have higher level science concepts, they will not get credited with the knowledge because they will be penalized due to reading difficulty.

Several linguistic structures have been identified as causing undue difficulty for hearing-impaired students. These include the conditionals (*if, then*), inferentials (*could, should*), comparatives (*greater than, less than*), negations (*not, without*), and low information pronouns (*it, something*). The SAT-HI vocabulary subtests contain items that incorporate, one or more of these linguistic structures. Consequently, the test results may be spuriously low because of the students' inability to deal with these structures.

The Grade Equivalent Score (GES) uses only hearing students as the reference group. Thus, the GES provides a method of defining pupil performance in terms of median public school grade level performance, and it is only useful when interpreted in this way. The average GES for third graders in one school can be compared with the performance of other third graders in other schools, providing a gross index of below-average, average, or above-average performance. Due to this fact, the GES has limited value in describing the academic performance of hearing-impaired students. Information indicating that a junior high school–aged hearing-impaired student does better than 35 percent of second-grade hearing children on a test based on a different curriculum is entirely useless. A comparison with hearing students may be important only in that it assesses the potential of deaf students. However, that a test designed for second-grade hearing children is even administered to junior high school–aged hearing-impaired students seems to already provide substantial comparative information.

Teacher-Made Tests

Standardized tests are not the only valid means of assessing students' current level of functioning. Teacher-made tests are valuable and legitimate means of measuring knowledge, comprehension, and progress.

Our lessons are based on our intent to teach a variety of specific skills and concepts. Therefore, the tests we design to measure learning will vary depending on what we are evaluating.

There are three types of teacher-made tests. One type is the pretest. This is given in an attempt to assess prior knowledge; the results should allow teachers to decide where instruction on a particular topic should begin if teaching is to be effective.

A second type of test provides the teacher with a way to assess ongoing learning. The reason for this type of testing is to determine whether or not instruction is effective or if it needs to be modified or revised. Ongoing assessment provides feedback to both the teacher and the student as to attained knowledge or skill. Well-planned and executed ongoing assessment can reveal weaknesses or areas of difficulty for the student and can result in a better learning situation for your students.

The third type of evaluation is developed by teachers at the conclusion of a specified learning period. It is designed to determine accurately the actual achievement attained during the course of study. How well the students met the goals is the measure of effective teaching. Final testing tells us if we actually taught what we thought we were teaching. Ideally, the students learned and will be able to demonstrate their new knowledge. If they can, we have been effective in teaching the specific skills or concepts that we wanted to teach.

Measurement Tools

The preparation of different types of evaluation requires planning. One of the most often used test formats is the paper-and-pencil test. This can take the form of homework, quizzes, exams, or term papers. If this is the type of test you want to use, be sure of exactly what you want the student to demonstrate. Term papers or essay tests require students to analyze and synthesize. Completion tests demand recall skills, while matching or multiple-choice tests require recognition skills. In constructing any type of paper-and-pencil tests, first define what it is you want to evaluate and what you are requiring of the students. Your decisions will be best made if they are based on your objectives.

Due to the reading and language problems suffered by many hearing-impaired children, other testing options are appropriate. Observation, class discussions, oral exams, or projects are all viable options for evaluating hearing-impaired students' learning. Allowing for the language limitations of hearing-impaired pupils, a teacher can organize and plan measurement options that will not place the students at a disadvantage when demonstrating their learning. These methods of assessing will help to eliminate anxiety and frustration on the students' part.

A final note of warning: keep testing and test results in proper perspective. Any particular test provides only one small sample of students' abilities. Several methods should be used, with a total picture drawn from many different attempts over time.

Summary

After pointing out all the negative aspects and cautions about testing, it is important to add that intelligence and achievement tests are useful if approached with caution and prudence.

The tests are of value to sort children out in rank order for purposes of grouping. They are also useful in demonstrating a child's achievement over a long period of time. The Hiskey-Nebraska, Leiter, and WISC-R all have been shown to be good predictors of academic success, and the Leiter seems to be sensitive to learning problems (Ratcliffe & Ratcliffe, 1979). The Performance scale of the WISC-R has been found to discriminate between high and low academic achievers. The Picture Arrangement, Block Design, and Coding subtests have been shown to correlate significantly with speech-reading ability. Therefore, these tests would be useful in developing individual programs instead of slotting hearing-impaired students into already existing programs.

The average deaf student is usually not ready to handle a commercial achievement test until age 7 or 8 (Gerweck & Ysseldyke, 1975). The administration of most tests before that age is not likely to provide much useful information. The question of who to test should not be taken lightly; it is necessary to consider the content of the tests as well as the age, language skills, mental condition, and physical ability of the student. Regardless of which tests are given, results should always be interpreted in terms of the total student. The role of test information can be maximized by the careful selection, administration, and interpretation of appropriate instruments. Those of us who are involved with decision-making in regard to programming for and teaching deaf children must be aware of the limitations of test instruments as well as the limitations of other personnel working with and testing the students.

CHAPTER
·6·

Implementation

*T*echniques used in implementing teaching strategies and materials should make use of a combination of the learner's senses, emotions, and/or motor functions. Available evidence on learning in deaf children emphasizes using concrete materials and experiences in instruction. Deaf children learn best when they are allowed to be actively involved in the learning process. When direct involvement or manipulation is not possible, using learners' previous experience to tie in or integrate new concepts and information is essential. Thus, the key is to build new material on past learning. Your teaching techniques should consider the learners' mental capacity and social, emotional, and physical development; the ability for learning to be utilized meaningfully by the students; the interest of the students; variety of presentation; provision for the progression from simple to complex knowledge and/or skills; reinforcement of previous learning; provision for individual instruction when possible; tasks at which the students can succeed; and means of evaluation to monitor, adjust, and improve the teaching process.

This chapter examines competencies in delivery of instruction, variety of activities provided, pacing of presentations, and feedback to facilitate and guide student learning, while considering the above concerns in implementing lessons.

Once you, the teacher, have identified instructional goals for any specific class, analyzed the tasks involved in mastering each skill or concept to be learned, and selected or modified appropriate materials, it is time to put the program into effect. Each classroom will have within it students who possess unique characteristics and who vary in their abilities to perform specific learning tasks.

Considerations for Making Decisions

Your instruction may differ greatly regarding the materials and the method of presentation you use, but the content will remain the same. You will be required to adapt instruction to fit the range of individual needs for your students. As no single approach will prove effective for all learners, you will need to determine each student's capabilities in order for your instruction to be beneficial to all pupils. This includes decisions about individual versus group instruction, pacing, types of activities used, and communication modes.

Both long-term goals and short-term objectives are determined by student characteristics and learning facts, including the following:

1. Age

2. Sex (boys and girls develop at different rates)

3. Physical makeup

4. Physical condition

5. Body chemistry

6. IQ/learning aptitude

7. Cognitive style

8. Anxiety level

9. Self-concept

10. Developmental needs

11. Level of aspiration

12. The need for achievement

13. The degree of independence

14. Availability of feedback

15. Physical characteristics of the learning environment

16. Teachers

17. Availability of materials

18. Number and characteristics of colearners

19. Available rewards and punishment

20. Acceptance signals

21. Communication skills

22. Socialization skills

23. The degree of hearing loss

24. Tolerance of others

25. Avoiding negative outcomes

Individual Versus Group Instruction

Your decision whether to conduct lessons to groups or individuals will be influenced by the capabilities of the pupils in your classroom. Students will possess different strengths and weaknesses in different areas. They will differ in what they already know, the amount of time they need to acquire new concepts and skills, and the communication methods by which they learn best. If you ignore the individual learning styles of your students, some of them will not learn. As a result, instructional strategies must correspond to the needs of each student involved in the learning environment. Remember that what works best for one individual may not be advantageous for another.

The practice of grouping by ability reflects an effort to maximize teaching time and often proves to be an appropriate technique. However, even with your best efforts to form groups based on similar levels of cognitive and academic functioning, some variance is still to be expected. For example, within each group, you will have to accommodate students who work at a faster rate than others. You will not want to limit or bore them; at the same time, you will not want to frustrate the slower working students. Additionally, each student will work at different rates on different subjects. Thus, pacing is an important factor in planning group work.

When individual teaching is required for some pupils in specific content or skill areas, the effective teacher must be prepared with additional work for the other students in the room. Too often, teachers resort to worksheets to keep students from being a distraction to their classmates, and these worksheets have no other value than to keep students busy. However, if not used just as busywork, worksheets can be useful practice aids; the practice they provide should be clearly related to academic goals and the student should understand their rationale and importance.

Instructional Strategies

Regardless of how you group students for any lesson, your teaching activities should be arranged to provide systematic, developmental instruction in a specific skill or concept.

Presentation of lessons usually takes place in three phases. First, the introductory phase provides students with the objectives of the lesson along with clear communication of your expectation of them in terms of eventual demonstration of mastery of the skill or concept. Information about what is to be done and how it is to be evaluated does much to relieve student anxiety.

Clear instructions are helpful to both the teacher and the students. Students who are able to work on their own with minimal teacher assistance can proceed without asking the teacher for directions about what to do next. This frees the teacher to provide individual guidance to those students who require it. For some students, a prepared list of expectations that they can check off may help them feel in control as well as help them see their own progress. This list can include behavioral as well as academic expectations. Behavioral rules can help eliminate distracting conduct as students complete their work and change activities.

The introduction also lays the groundwork for the lesson. It defines and offers identifying attributes of the new concepts or skills and reviews previous learning in a way that relates the new material to what has already been learned. This is helpful in providing the students with a framework for understanding the new information, and it helps reduce fear of the unknown and of anticipated failure, which is often a part of a hearing-impaired child's experience. If new material is made meaningful for the students, their ability to remember will be enhanced. The introduction phase is also the appropriate time to teach the vocabulary necessary to ensure meaningfulness of a new concept or skill. Several demonstrations should be used to establish meaning.

Phase two is the content phase. It involves the actual presentation of material. Instruction should be designed and presented in ways that will foster and improve student performance in specified tasks. Techniques used should vary within each lesson in order to accommodate all needs within your classroom, with consideration given to differences in the information-processing capabilities of your students. You will also find differences in the students' abilities to concentrate and retain information. Therefore, the amount of material presented and the rate of input must be controlled to establish learning.

Instruction should begin at the students' entry level with a carefully controlled sequence. An effective teacher will present many examples of new concepts and will provide several opportunities to practice new skills. The teacher will help students participate in their learning. When necessary, demonstrations are provided by the teacher to support and reinforce understanding by the students. Students can be distracted and miss important steps or points. Demonstrations should be repeated as often as necessary. The modeling of procedures can be an acceptable and effective method of instruction.

Teachers who are sensitive to the needs of hearing-impaired students will employ a variety of visual aids to assist the comprehension of abstract concepts by providing concrete support. For example, graphics, charts, posters, photographs, films, transparencies, books, and student-made materials are usually available or easily made and should be age- and level-appropriate.

Manipulatives provide concrete aid in developing concepts while providing hands-on discovery learning opportunities.

Students enjoy opportunities to show off their learning. Opportunities to discuss experiences, along with effective correcting, prompting, and modeling techniques, aid academic understanding and learning without damaging students' self-concept. Planned practice time promotes student progress and achievement.

The teacher should also provide immediate positive feedback to reinforce achievement or to correct errors. This eliminates students guessing or assuming the correctness or incorrectness of their responses.

Teachers must never assume comprehension. Instead, they should ask frequent, well-formed questions to verify student comprehension. Questions must be answered by demonstration of understanding, not simply *yes* or *no* responses. If asked, "Do you understand?" most students will answer "yes" rather than appear slow or stupid even though they may be completely lost. Instead, teachers should ask for an explanation or restatement of what was just covered.

A component of the second phase is shifting instructional activities during the lesson. Competent teachers make shifts easily and smoothly from one activity to another with minimal transition time to assure continuity.

The third phase, closure, allows the teacher to accurately determine what learning has occurred or what objectives have been reached. This involves summarizing information verbally with positive examples. The closure phase also provides ways to identify what each student, individually, understands as a result of the instruction. The correct assessment of each student's progress will help the teacher establish the entry level at which to begin instruction for the next lesson. Hearing-impaired children are not proficient in questioning techniques due to a lack of experience in complex questions. Teach your students to ask questions when they require clarification or need further explanation to understand a point. In this manner, you will be able to identify their knowledge, or lack of it, to further insure finding the correct instructional level for subsequent lessons.

Evaluation

Although evaluation of a lesson is an integral part of the second and third levels, it is important enough to deserve separate attention. Correct assessment by the teacher of what has or hasn't been learned leads to the adjustment and modification of materials and/or instructional techniques.

Evaluation can and should take many forms. To be effective, teachers should provide frequent formal and informal assessment of pupil progress in order to determine achievement of academic goals and objectives. Directed discussions, quizzes, or demonstrations by students can provide the information necessary to allow the teacher to decide where to begin subsequent instruction. If the established goals haven't been reached, the teacher must examine strategies and the materials used to make decisions about reteaching. Changes may be required at any point in the instructional sequence if a breakdown in learn-ing is found. Students also benefit from evaluation. If presented in a way that doesn't intimidate or embarrass them, evaluation helps them realize and be recognized for their attainment of skills or knowledge.

Communication Method

Another important implementation method has to do with the mode of input. The general philosophy of the school will determine if you use oral instruction only within your classroom or if you use any of the total communication methods.

It is not the intent of this chapter to promote one method over the other. Respect for the needs and integrity of the individual student will guide deciding which communication mode to use with which student. Language ability should be the major consideration, as language is a critical component for educational achievement. The approach used should reflect the students' communication capabilities, including expressive *and* receptive skills. After all, it is important both to comprehend and produce. Directions, information, explanations, and ques-tioning are all parts of instruction and must be easily understood and expressed by the students. The ease in the understanding of abstract concepts, through language, is achieved is a primary educational concern and determines the successes or failures of the hearing-impaired child.

Summary

The manner in which a teacher implements instruction in any classroom is determined largely by the ability to judge students' capabilities accurately. Instruction should begin at the students' entry level. Grouping by ability level may be used rather than teaching to individuals in an effort to maximize time constraints. New concepts and skills are introduced by defining attributes and tying them into previous learning. Vocabulary and language structures necessary to ensure meaningfulness must be taught and used in ways to verify understanding by the students. If new material is made meaningful for the students, their ability to remember will be enhanced.

Examples and/or demonstrations must be provided along with visual aids to enhance understanding of abstract concepts by use of concrete materials. Examples should be repeated if such repetition is needed by students. Students should be allowed to become active participants in their learning. Teacher talk or lecture should be kept to a minimum so students have opportunities to learn by doing and to demonstrate their knowledge. Pacing of a lesson should be controlled to accommodate the processing and memory abilities of individual students. Ongoing evaluation is also a part of implementing. This provides feedback for both the teacher and students, which will direct change or modification of the lesson to foster continued learning. Where learning breaks down, the problem must be assessed by the teacher in order to determine where and how to reteach or where to start the next lesson.

Examples of
Rewritten Lessons*

Rationale for Selecting Text

1. The stories appear to be of high interest. They are appealing in the following aspects:
   a. Adventure
   b. Emotion
   c. Mystery
   d. Science fiction
   e. Age-appropriateness
   f. Universal interests, crossing cultures and socio-economic classes

*Excerpt from "The People in the Castle" from the book *Not What You Expected* by Joan Aiken. Copyright © 1974 by Joan Aiken. Reprinted by permission of Doubleday, a division of Bantam, Doubleday, Dell Publishing Group, Inc.

2. Classic literature is represented, often portraying lives of real and interesting people, relating historical happenings, and describing places of intrigue.

3. Functional and skill-oriented reading is alternated with high-interest stories.

4. Plays and poetry are interspersed.

5. General directives appear quite explicit throughout the book, with special vocabulary defined at the bottom of pages.

6. The illustrations are as follows:
   a. Colorful
   b. Emotional
   c. Action filled
   d. Clearly defined

Rationale for Selecting Workbook

1. The format is uncluttered and easy to follow visually.

2. The directives are concise, and there are no more than two separate activities per page.

Rationale for Selecting Vocabulary Book

1. The vocabulary book is separate.

2. The format contains the following:
    a. A repetitive structure for each story, including
        1. Glossary words
        2. Newly introduced words
        3. Vocabulary activity
    b. Clear visual presentation
3. Vocabulary activities are presented in a game format:
    a. Crossword puzzles
    b. Anagrams
    c. Context
    d. Sentence writing
    e. Scrambled words
    f. Multiple choice

Original Story

"Will you bring it?" she said, solving his problem. "My father will be glad to see you."

"Of course. I'll bring it tomorrow evening."

Again she gravely inclined her head, and turning, was gone, though whether by the door or window he could not be sure.

He crossed to the window and stood for some time staring up at the black bulk of the castle on the thorn-covered hill, before returning to his desk and the unfinished sentence. He left the curtains open.

Next morning, if it had not been for the prescription lying on his desk, he would have thought that the incident had been a dream. Even as he took the slip along to Boots to have the medicine made up he wondered if the white-coated woman there would suddenly tell him that he was mad.

That evening, dusk was falling as the last of his surgery patients departed. He went down and locked the large gates and then started the long climb up the steps to the castle. It was lighter up on the side of the knoll. The thorns and brambles grew so high that he could see nothing but the narrow stairway in front of him. When he reached the top, he looked down and saw his own house below, and the town with its crooked roofs running to the foot of the hill, and the river wriggling away to the sea. Then he turned and walked under the arch into the great hall of the castle.

The first thing he noticed was the scent of lime. There was a big lime tree which, in the daytime, grew in the middle of the grass carpeting the great hall. He could not see the tree, but why was a lime tree blossoming in October?

It was dark inside, and he stood hesitating, afraid to step forward into the gloom, when he felt a hand slipped into his. It was a thin hand, very cool; it gave him a gentle tug and he moved forward, straining his eyes to try and make out who was leading him. Then, as if the pattern in a kaleidoscope had cleared, his eyes flickered and he began to see.

There were lights grouped round the walls in pale clusters, and below them, down the length of the hall, sat a large and shadowy assembly; he could see the glint of light here and there on armour, or on a gold buckle or the jewel in a headdress as somebody moved.

At the top of the hall, on a dais, sat a royal figure, cloaked and stately, but the shadows lay so thick in between that he could see no more. But his guide plucked him forward; he now saw that it was Helen, in her white dress with a gold belt and bracelets. She smiled at him gravely and indicated that he was to go up and salute the King.

Paragraph One (Original)

"Will you bring it?" she said, solving his problem. "My father will be glad to see you."

CONSTRUCTIONS

"That" clause reduced (*That* solved his problem)— "participle"—"solving his problem"

PARAGRAPH ONE (REWRITE)

"Will you bring it?" Helen said. "My father will be glad to see you."

Paragraph Two (Original)

"Of course. I'll bring it tomorrow evening."

CONSTRUCTIONS

No direct referent as to who is speaking.

PARAGRAPH TWO (REWRITE)

"Of course," the doctor replied, "I'll bring it tomorrow evening.

Paragraph Three (Original)

Again she gravely inclined her head, and turning, was gone, though whether by the door or window he could not be sure.

VOCABULARY

gravely

inclined

whether

or

CONSTRUCTIONS

Embedded question

Either/or concept—"whether by the door or window"

Sequence—sentence has multiple constructions and clauses

PARAGRAPH THREE (REWRITE)

Again she gravely inclined her head. She turned and suddenly disappeared. Did she leave through the door? Did she leave through the window? He could not be sure.

Paragraph Four (Original)

He crossed to the window and stood for some time staring up at the black bulk of the castle on the thorn-covered hill, before returning to his desk and the unfinished sentence. He left the curtains open.

VOCABULARY

some time

bulk

thorn-covered

unfinished

CONSTRUCTIONS

Referent unclear, using participle "staring"

Sequence—first sentence has multiple constructions and clauses

"Time" clause at end position—"participle"—"before [he returned] returning to his desk"

Particle—left. . .open"

PARAGRAPH FOUR (REWRITE)

He crossed to the window and stood for some time. He stared up at the huge dark castle on the thorn-covered hill. Then he returned to his desk and the unfinished sentence. He did not shut the curtains. He asked himself, "Was that woman really here? Was I dreaming?"

Paragraph Five (Original)

Next morning, if it had not been for the prescription lying on his desk, he would have thought that the incident had been a dream. Even as he took the slip along to Boots to have the medicine made up he wondered if the white-coated woman there would suddenly tell him that he was mad.

VOCABULARY

prescription

incident

mad

to have

FIGURATIVE LANGUAGE OR IDIOMS

Referent unclear—"backward pronoun"—"it"

"That" clause reduction (. . .the prescription *that* lay on his desk)—"participle" as adjective—"[that was] lying on his desk"

"That" clause—"complement" as direct object—"(that the incident had been a dream)"

"Time" clause—"even as he took the slip along to Boots" (present "even")

Particle—"made up"

"That" clause—"complement" as direct object—"that he was mad"

PARAGRAPH FIVE (REWRITE)

The next morning the doctor looked for the prescription and it was on his desk. He had *not* been dreaming. Now he worried about something else. Would the druggist believe him? (Helen had really been there!) The doctor was not mad!

Paragraph Six (Original)

That evening, dusk was falling as the last of his surgery patients departed. He went down and locked the large gates and then started the long climb up the steps to the castle. It was lighter up on the side of the knoll. The thorns and brambles grew so high that he could see nothing but the narrow stairway in front of him. When he reached the top, he looked down and saw his own house below, and the town with its crooked roofs running to the foot of the hill, and the river wriggling away to the sea. Then he turned and walked under the arch into the great hall of the castle.

VOCABULARY

dusk

surgery

departed

knoll

brambles

running

reached

wriggling

arch

great hall

FIGURATIVE LANGUAGE AND IDIOMS

dusk was falling

nothing but

crooked roofs running to the foot of the hill

the river wriggling away to the sea

CONSTRUCTIONS

"Time" clause—"as the last of his surgery patients departed"

Sequence—"He went down and locked the large gates and then started the long climb up the steps to the castle."

Referent unclear—"it"

"That" clause as adverb—"that he could see nothing but the narrow stairway in front of him"

"Time" clause—"when he reached the top"

PARAGRAPH SIX CONTINUED (CONSTRUCTIONS)

Sequence—"he looked down and saw his own house below, and the town with its crooked roofs running to the foot of the hill, and the river wriggling away to the sea"

"That" clause (reduced)—"participle" as adjective—"[that ran] running" to the foot of the hill"

"That" clause (reduced)—"participle" as adjective—"[that wriggled] wriggling away to the sea"

Sequence—"walked under the arch into the great hall of the castle"

PARAGRAPH SIX (REWRITE)

That evening his last patient left at dusk. He went down the hill and locked the large gates. Then he started the long climb up the steps to the castle. He climbed higher, and the side of the knoll became lighter. The thorns and brambles grew high; he could see only the narrow stairway in front of him. He reached the top of the steps and looked down at his own house below. He saw many sloping, crooked roofs. Altogether, the roofs looked like a long, long "slide" down the hill. The river looked like a long, wriggly snake. Then he turned and walked into the great hall of the castle.

Paragraph Seven (Original)

The first thing he noticed was the scent of lime. There was a big lime tree which, in the daytime, grew in the middle of the grass carpeting the great hall. He could not see the tree, but why was a lime tree blossoming in October?

VOCABULARY

scent

CONSTRUCTIONS

"That" clause (reduced) as adjective—"[that] he noticed"

"That" clause as adjective—"which, in the daytime, grew in the middle of the grass"

"That" clause (reduction)—"participle" as adjective—"[that carpeted] carpeting the great hall"

PARAGRAPH SEVEN (REWRITE)

He noticed the scent of lime. There was a big lime tree. It grew from the grassy floor of the great hall. Why was the lime tree blossoming in October?

Paragraph Eight (Original)

It was dark inside, and he stood hesitating, afraid to step forward into the gloom, when he felt a hand slipped into his. It was a thin hand, very cool; it gave him a gentle tug and he moved forward, straining his eyes to try and make out who was leading him. Then, as if the pattern in a kaleidoscope had cleared, his eyes flickered and he began to see.

VOCABULARY

hesitating

gloom

straining

kaleidoscope

flickered

FIGURATIVE LANGUAGE AND IDIOMS

as if a pattern in a kaleidoscope had cleared

CONSTRUCTIONS

"Time" clause—"when he felt a hand"

"That" clause (reduced)—"[that] slipped into his"

Referent unclear—"his"

Referent unclear—"it"

Particle—"make out"

Indirect question—"who was leading him"

Sequence—all sentences have difficult constructions in sequence

PARAGRAPH EIGHT (REWRITE)

It was dark inside. He hesitated because he was afraid to step forward into the gloom. Then he felt a hand; it slipped into his hand. The hand was thin and very cool. It tugged gently and he moved forward. He strained his eyes to see. Whose hand was this? He flickered his eyes; then he began to make out this "weird-looking" place.

Paragraph Nine Original

There were lights grouped round the walls in pale clusters, and below them, down the length of the hall, sat a large and shadowy assembly; he could see the glint of light here and there on armour, or on a gold buckle or the jewel in a headdress as somebody moved.

VOCABULARY

pale

clusters

glint

headdress

FIGURATIVE LANGUAGE AND IDIOMS
shadowy assembly

PARAGRAPH NINE (REWRITE)

There were groups of pale lights on the walls and below him. Many people were on both sides of this long, dark great hall. He could see glints of light from shiny objects. He saw armour and jeweled headdresses.

Paragraph Ten (Original)

At the top of the hall, on a dais, sat a royal figure, cloaked and stately, but the shadows lay so thick in between that he could see no more. But his guide plucked him forward; he now saw that it was Helen, in her white dress with a gold belt and bracelets. She smiled at him gravely and indicated that he was to go up and salute the King.

VOCABULARY
dais

figure

cloaked

stately

plucked

indicated

CONSTRUCTIONS

Sequence—the first sentence is difficult due to an inverted subject, the vocabulary used, and the use of modifiers (prepositional, participle, adverbial) and clauses

"That" clause ("that" is used in place of the conjunctive adverb, therefore in a coordinating role)—"that he could see no more"

"That" clause complement used as direct object—"that it was Helen"

"That" clause complement used as direct object—"that he was to go up and salute the King"

Particle—"had on"

PARAGRAPH TEN (REWRITE)

He saw a royal person on a throne at the end of the hall. The room was shadowy and dim. Someone pulled him forward; it was Helen. She had on her white dress with the gold belt and bracelets. She smiled gravely at him. She pointed toward the King.

Comments: Vocabulary Development

The assumed "new" vocabulary from the basal reader should be utilized to assess the vocabulary of the student(s) at the beginning of each semester preceding the semester of its presentation or at least, at the start of the semester of its presentation (see Table 1). Some of the words in the story were retained and others were deleted; however, a number of the words that were deleted from the story should be taught during eighth-grade vocabulary development as they are considered to be commonly used words. Whether or not these words were taught the semester previously, they should be used diagnostically at the beginning of the semester.

The vocabulary words that are still unclear in meaning, should be taught or retaught and used as much as possible in the context of school activities, including theme writing, learning games, day-to-day conversation, etc. Children should make dictionaries during the semester to have ready access to these word meanings for use during reading, game activities, and otherwise. Lists should be sent home for parents so that they can use these words contextually with their children. The words should be reviewed at the beginning of the semester and before each reading lesson in which they are found. The words should then be reviewed before the appropriate reading lesson, in the exact story context and with vocabulary worksheets and discussion.

Some suggestions for vocabulary activities might include the following:

TABLE 1.

Vocabulary, Figurative Language, and Idioms Used in the Story

Paragraph Number	Retained Vocabulary	Deleted Vocabulary
One	gravely inclinded	whether...or (deaf children will have problems with this construction
Four	some time thorn-covered unfinished	bulk (rather uncommon)
Five	prescription mad (crazy)	incident* to have (meaning "to request")*
Six	dusk knoll brambles reached (came to) wriggly "great hall"	surgery (meaning is uncommon) departed* running (multiple meaning)* arch dusk was falling nothing but* foot of the hill* river wriggling
Seven	scent	
Eight	hesitated gloom strained flickered	kaleidoscope*
Nine	pale glint headdress	clusters shadowy assembly
Ten		dais figure* cloaked stately plucked indicated*

*These words, though deleted, should be addressed during vocabulary development.

Card games such as Rummy or Go Fish

Crossword puzzles

Anagrams

Word downs (like spell downs)

Acrostics: for example, the first letter of each word must spell a word when all answers are seen

Analogy games (synonyms or antonyms): for example, a series game—*hot, cold, black*

Category games, played like Rummy and color-coded

Context worksheets and games: might be played like Go Fish with the sentence on one side of the card and the word fitting in the blank on the opposite side of the card.

Phrases:
1. "Weird-looking place" "the castle looked weird."
2. "Jeweled headdresses" "headbands made of jewelry."
3. Particle "had on" was retained because hearing-impaired children utilize this verb at young age.

References

Bernstein, D. K., and Tiegerman, E. (1985). *Language and communcation disorders in children*. Columbus, OH: Charles E. Merrill Publishing Company.

Brannon, J. and Murray, T. (1966). The spoken syntax of normal, hard of hearing, and deaf children. *Journal of Speech and Hearing Science, 9,* 604–610.

Brill, R. G. (1962). The relationship of Wechsler's IQs to academic achievement among deaf students. *Exceptional Child, 28,* 315–321.

Brill, R. (1977). Problems in testing and evaluating deaf children. Washington, D.C.: MSSD Publications (Gallaudet College).

Clarke, B. R., and Stewart, D. A. (1986). Reflections on language programs for the hearing impaired. *Journal of Special Education, 20,* 153–165.

Cohen, B. K. (1980). Emotionally disturbed hearing-impaired children: A review of the literature. *American Annals of the Deaf, 125,* 1040–1048.

Conrad, R. (1979). *The deaf school child: Language and cognitive function*. London: Harper and Row.

Davis, J. (1974). Performance of young hearing impaired children on a test of basic concepts. *Journal of Speech and Hearing Research, 17,* 342–351.

Dicker, L. (1977). Psychological aspects of deafness. *The Wisconsin Association of the Deaf Pilot,* Fall Issue.

DiFrancesca, S. (1972). Academic achievement results of a national testing program for hearing impaired students. Washington, D.C.: Gallaudet College.

Furth, H. G. (1966). A comparison of reading test norms of deaf and hearing children. *American Annals of the Deaf, 111,* 461–462.

Furth, H. G. (1966). *Thinking without language.* New York: Free Press.

Furth, H. G. (1964). Research with the deaf: Implications for language and cognition. *Psychological Bulletin, 62,* 145–165.

Furth, H. G., and Youniss, J. (1971). Formal operations and language: A comparison of deaf and hearing subjects. *International Journal of Psychology, 6,* 49–64.

Gentile, M. and McCarthy, B. (1973). Additional handicapping conditions among hearing impaired students, U.S.: 1971–72 (Series D, #14). Washington, D.C.: Gallaudet College Office of Demographic Studies.

Gerwech, S., and Ysseldyke, J. (1975). Limitations of current psychological practices for the intellectual assessment of the hearing impaired: A response to the Levine study. *Volta Review, 77,* 243–248.

Glover, J., Bruning, R., and Filbeck, R. (1983). *Educational psychology, Principles and applications.* Boston, MA: Little, Brown and Co.

Griswold, E., and Commings, J. (1974). The expressive vocabulary of preschool deaf children. *American Annals of the Deaf, 119,* 16–28.

Hammermeister, F. K. (1971). Reading achievement in deaf adults. *American Annals of the Deaf, 116,* 25–28.

Hiskey, M. S. (1956). A study of the intelligence of deaf and hearing children. *American Annals of the Deaf, 101,* 329–339.

Jensema, C. (1975). The relationship between academic achievement and the demographic characteristics of hearing impaired children and youth. Series R, Number 2, Washington, D.C.: Gallaudet College Office of Demographic Studies.

Jensema, C. (1980). Considerations in utilizing achievement tests for the hearing impaired. *American Annals of the Deaf, 125,* 495–498.

Jensema, C. and Trybus, R. (1978). Communication patterns and educational achievement of hearing impaired students, Series T, Number 2, Washington, D.C.: Gallaudet College Office of Demographic Studies.

Kretschmer, R. and Kretschmer, L. (1978). *Language development and intervention with hearing impaired.* Baltimore: University Park Press.

Kretschmer, R. E. and Quigley, S. P. (1982). *The education of deaf children: Issues, theory & practice.* Baltimore, MD: University Park Press.

Lenneberg, E. H. (1967). *Biological Foundations of Language.* New York: Wiley.

Levine, E. (1974). Psychological tests and practices with the deaf. *Volta Review, 76,* 298–319.

Levine, E. S. (1960). *The psychology of deafness.* New York: Columbia University Press.

Maslow, A. H. (1970). *Motivation and personality* (2nd ed.). New York: Harper and Row.

Meadow, K. (1973). Indentity crisis: Special problem of the deaf child and his parents. *The California News,* 1–4.

Meadow, K. P., and Trybus, R. J. (1979). Behavioral and emotional problems of deaf children: An overview. In L. Bradford and W. Harly (eds.), *Hearing and hearing impairment.* New York: Grune & Stratton.

Meadow, K. P. Greenberg, M. T., Erteng, C., and Carmichael, H. (1981). Interactions of deaf mothers and deaf preschool children: Comparisons with three other groups of deaf and hearing dyads. *American Annals of the Deaf, 126,* 454–468.

Miera, M. P. (1962). The use of the Arthur Adaptation of the Leiter International Performance Scale and Nebraska Test of Learning Aptitude with preschool deaf children. *American Annals of the Deaf, 107,* 224–228.

Mindel, E., and Vernon, M. (1971). *They grow in silence.* Silver Spring, MD: National Association of the Deaf.

Moores, D. (1978). *Educating the deaf: Psychology, principles and practices.* Boston, MA: Houghton Mifflin.

Moores, D. (1978). Current research and theory with the deaf:

Educational implications. In L. Liben (ed.), *Deaf children: Developmental perspectives*. New York: Academic Press.

Myklebust, H. R. (1948). Clinical psychology and children with impaired hearing. *Volta Review, 50,* 55–60.

Nicolosi, L., Harryman, E., and Kresheck, J. (1978). *Terminology of communication disorders: Speech, language, hearing.* Baltimore, MD: Williams and Wilkins.

Pintner, R. (1933). Emotional stability of the hard of hearing. *Journal of Genetic Psychology, 43,* 293–309.

Power, H., and Quigley, S. (1973). Deaf children's acquisition of passive voice. *Journal of Speech and Hearing Research, 16,* 5–11.

Quigley, S. P., and Kretschmer, R. E. (1982). *The education of deaf children.* Baltimore: University Park Press.

Quigley, S., and Power, D. (1972). *The development of syntactic structures in the language of deaf children.* Urbana, IL: Institute for Research of Exceptional Children.

Quigley, S. P., and Power, D. J. (1979). *TSA syntax program.* Beaverton, OR: Dorma, Inc.

Quigley, S. P., Power, D. J., and Steinkamp, M. W. (1977). The language structure of deaf children. *The Volta Review, 79,* 73–84.

Quigley, S. P., Smith, N. L., and Wilbur, R. B. (1974). Comprehension of relativized sentences by deaf students. *Journal of Speech and Hearing Research, 17,* 325–341.

Ratcliffe, K., and Ratcliffe, M. (1979). The Leiter Scales: A review of validity findings. *American Annals of the Deaf, 124,* 38–44.

Reed, V. A. (1986). *An introduction to children with language disorders.* New York: Macmillan.

Rosenstein, J. (1961). Perception, cognition and language in deaf children. *Exceptional Child, 28,* 276–284.

Rudner, L. (1978). Using standardized tests with the hearing impaired: The problem of bias. *Volta Review, 80,* 31–40.

Schein, J. D., and Delk, M. T. (1974). *The deaf population of the United States.* Silver Spring, MD: National Association of the Deaf.

Schildroth, A. D. (1980). Residential schools for deaf students in the U.S., 1970–1978. *American Annals of the Deaf, 125,* 80–91.

Schlesinger, H. S., and Meadow, K. P. (1972). *Sound and sign: Childhood deafness and mental health.* Berkeley: University of California Press.

Stout Vocational Rehabilitation Institute (June 1960). *Interpreter services for deaf clients*. Stout, WI: University of Wisconsin.

Tomlinson-Keasey, C., and Kelly, R. (1974). The development of thought processes in deaf children. *American Annals of the Deaf, 119*, 693–700.

Trybus, R. J., and Karchmer, K. A. (1977). School achievement scores of hearing impaired children: National data on achievement status and growth patterns. *American Annals of the Deaf, 122*, 62–69.

Vernon, M. (1968). Fifty years of research on the intelligence of deaf and hard-of-hearing children. A review of literature and discussion of implications. *Journal of Rehabilitation of the Deaf, 1*, 1–2.

Vernon, M. (1969). Sociological and pathological factors associated with hearing loss. *Journal of Speech and Hearing Disorders, 12*, 541–563.

Whorf, B. (1956). *Language, thought, and reality*. Cambridge, MA: Massachusetts Institute of Technology Press.

Wilcox, J., and Tobin, H. (1974). Linguistic performance of hard of hearing and normal hearing children. *Journal of Speech and Hearing Research, 17*, 286–292.

Wlodkowski, R. J. (1984). *Motivation and teaching*. Washington, D.C.: National Education Association.

Youniss, J. (1964). Concept transfer as a function of shifts, ages and deafness. *Child Development, 35*, 695–700.

Deaf Heroes

Albronda, M. (1980). *Douglas Tilden: Portait of a Deaf Sculptor*. Silver Spring, MD: National Association of the Deaf.

Burlingame, R. (1964). *Out of silence into sound: the life of Alexander Graham Bell*. New York, NY: The Macmillan Company.

De Gering, E. (1964). *Gallaudet: Friend of the Deaf*. New York, NY: David McKay Company.

Gannon, J. (1981). *Deaf Heritage: A narrative history of deaf America*. Silver Spring, MD: The National Association of the Deaf.

Huston, C. (1974). *Deaf Smith: Incredible Texas Spy*. Waco, TX: Texian Press.

Panara, J. and Panara, J. *Great deaf Americans.* Silver Spring, MD: T. J. Publishers.

Powers, H. (1972). *Signs of silence: Bernard Bragg and the National Theatre of the Deaf.* New York, NY: Dodd, Mead and Co.

Woods, W. (1973). *The Forgotten People.* St. Petersburg, FL: Dixie Press.

Sources for Low-Level, High-Interest Material

Dormac, Inc.; P.O. Box 1699; Beaverton, OR 97075–1699.

Gallaudet College Press; 800 Florida Avenue NE; Washington D.C. 20002.

Now Age Books Illustrated; Pendulum Press; West Haven, CT 06516.

Opportunities for Learning; 20417 Nordoff St.; Dept. 3 BRS; Chatsworth, CA 91311.

Reader's Digest Services, Inc. (Skill Builder Books); Pleasantville, NY 10570.

Subject Index